Christmas Meditations
on the
Twelve Holy Days

December 26 – January 6

Words and Art by
Merry C. Battles

authorHOUSE™

1663 LIBERTY DRIVE, SUITE 200
BLOOMINGTON, INDIANA 47403
(800) 839-8640
WWW.AUTHORHOUSE.COM

First published by AuthorHouse 04/18/05

ISBN: 1-4208-1572-5 (e)
ISBN: 1-4208-1571-7 (sc)

Library of Congress Control Number: 2004099448

Printed in the United States of America
Bloomington, Indiana

This book is printed on acid-free paper.

DEDICATION

I dedicate this book to those in my family
who have gone before me…
my beautiful sisters Marjorie and Donna,
who showed me love and great guidance,
and my mother and father,
who also taught me how to love.
Their presence in this life and the next
has been deeply appreciated.
I will love them forever!

ACKNOWLEDGEMENTS

My gratitude goes to my "sister," editor, and friend, Gloria Hicks, who helped me through the writing of this book. Her hours of punctuating and polishing of this manuscript have helped to bring it to birth.

Many thanks to Nicole Bottoms in her efforts in putting this book together on the computer and in scanning my artwork.

I send great appreciation to my daughter Hallae for her unending love and help. My thanks to her husband Ulrik and my grandsons for always being there for me.

Love to my two nephews who will always have a tender place in my heart.

Love to my dear friends and "sisters" who have encouraged me in my work.

Some of my poems were not actually written during the holy days. I have shared them with you because they would be beautiful additions to your meditations.

My limitless admiration goes to my earthly teachers and to my teachers on the other side of the "veil."

TABLE OF CONTENTS

v

FOREWORD

In reading this book, I found it a wonderful way to help the reader get to the heart of the Christmas season. Linking each zodiacal sign to each of the twelve holy days of Christmas to each of the twelve disciples and also connecting to a spiritual center in the physical body, aligning with a spiritual attainment and a thought meditation is a very spiritual connection which will help the reader further up the spiritual path as each day goes on.

This will truly help the reader realize that celebrating Christmas is much more than the simple exchange of gifts. As the wonderful author, Merry Battles, tells us, it is one of the few times of the year when the Divine Light is especially, intensely being sent down to this Mother Earth of ours and all the living beings thereon, including you and me.

This wonderful book presents to us a way to use this important time of the year to evolve spiritually as we also let the White Light into every part of our body. There is also wonderful poetry and artwork which help to convey this important message. I hope you find this book as useful and as fabulous as I have.

Dr. Sita E. Chaney
Astara
Upland, California

INTRODUCTION

This book is a compilation of twenty-six years of my personal dedication to the twelve holy days of Christmas. The continuation of Christmas starts on December 26 through January 6. It's very special to continue celebrating when most of the world believes it is over. For this reason I always keep my Christmas tree up until after the sixth.

Christmas has always been a very special time for me because Christmas Eve is my birthday. My mother named me Merry Christina. Somehow she didn't pay attention to our last name. Merry Battles, that is how it has always been. I like the irony, the yin and yang of it. Although I've had many battles, in the end they have turned out merry.

I started this practice in 1977 when I officially started walking "the path" (the sacred path). When learning about the spiritual side of life becomes one's greatest joy, you have stepped onto the path. I was always interested in spiritual things, ideas, and thoughts about the other worlds. I realized only a few years ago that within just three months I started my massage work, I took my first metaphysics class, and my sister Donna was diagnosed with terminal cancer. I began my physical study of the body along with the study of the Spirit.

About a year before this I went to a fund raising party at the airport. Donna was involved with the "Retreads," a group of people who were in wheelchairs. Two planes were parked in a hangar while a cocktail party was going on inside. A local Metaphysical church donated their time for some psychic readings. While waiting for my reading, I was sitting in an airplane seat sipping my first cocktail. A man who was giving psychometry readings was sitting near me. I started to feel funny, a little light headed and dizzy, and thought "What in the world is going on?" When it was finally my turn, I gave him a ring. He sat there and held it for a few moments to see if he could pick up some impressions from it. The first words he said were, "Sometimes I feel like a Queen." Well sometimes I did, but then other times I felt rotten. He told me I had many jewels in my crown but that they were cloudy. (We all receive spiritual "jewels" for our many lessons learned. They can be in our "breastplate" or our "Crown.") He also told me that my daughter Hallae, who was four at the time, was my mother in another lifetime. That sounded right; she was always mothering me.

About half an hour later, my sister Marjorie came running up to me. "When you left the plane, the man who was doing readings jumped up to say, 'Wait! Wait!'" I saw him a few minutes later and walked up to him. "I understand you were looking for me?" Lee said, "Do you remember me?" "You don't mean from this lifetime, do you?" He shook his head no, and added that we knew each other in many lifetimes. I sat there for a few minutes and tried to remember. "I feel like I was very close to you, that you were my brother." Lee gave me his card, and told me that if I remembered or needed him, to call him.

One year later I needed him. It was very early one Sunday morning. Hallae had been having some bad chest congestion on and off for a few months. I woke up to her wheezing and having difficulty breathing. My first and only thought was to call Lee. He told me he knew I was going to call, that he was going into church but that he would call me later. While I was waiting for him, a neighbor came in and told me I should take her to the doctor. My intuition told me to wait for Lee's call, and it was a good thing I did. "Instead of lamenting over Hallae, saying and feeling 'Oh my baby, my poor baby,' see her as well today. See her running and jumping and playing." He asked me if I had been upset lately. When I said yes, Lee said that Hallae was feeling everything that was going on with me. She was like a bank, bringing in all that I was feeling and multiplying it like interest. He had known exactly how I acted when she got sick!

For the rest of the afternoon I did what Lee had told me to do - I saw Hallae as well. I kept going in and checking on her for a few hours. At one point she asked me, "Did your friend leave?" About four in the afternoon, she got up, came out in the living room, asked for some dinner. She was about 80% better. I couldn't believe it! It was like a mini miracle!

The next day I asked her to explain what she had meant about my friend being there. "There was a man here and he was in a red dress. He was crying, he was moving his hand back and forth, he kissed you and me, and then he left." I saw Lee a few days later and asked him if he had come that day. "No, I did not come. You had an unconditional call for help and someone came in Spirit to assist you." For years after I could not understand why the man was moving his hands back and forth. A friend finally realized that the man was clearing the air of dust.

We are linked to our children with invisible gossamer threads. They feel everything we feel and more. Our thoughts affect them; our moods affect them every minute of the day. Starting in the womb, then as infants and young children, and probably for the rest of their lives, our children are connected to us. As my mother said, "It's a lifetime sentence." And I say, now I get to even worry about the grandchildren!

Lee was starting some classes a few weeks later. I attended these classes every week for two years. It was during this time that my sister Donna was diagnosed. Every week I would go to class and feel that I was almost infecting my classmates with how sad I felt. I did not know that I had any inner strength. I would pray for it and bathe my self mentally in the color red. That whole time I saw Donna as well. A few months before she died, I started having dreams that she was not going to make it. Seeing her as well was my will for her, not God's will. At the end of her life, I knew that there was some reason for her suffering - I didn't know what it was, but I knew there was a purpose. I realized: what an Ace to have in Heaven!

I started my meditation practice the year of all these events. The inspiration for my work came from the book *Mystery of the Christos* by Corinne Heline. In the book, each of the twelve holy days is assigned to one of the Zodiacal Hierarchies and its accompanying solar dates. The twelve spiritual centers of the physical body are seen illumined. Jesus's twelve disciples preside, one each day, with a passage from the Bible. By the twelfth night, our whole body is lit up like a glorious Christmas tree. Jesus chose His disciples because they represented every aspect of humanity. The twelve signs of the Zodiac are the archetypal cosmic patterns of all human behavior, so to assign the disciples to a sign of the Zodiac is a natural progression.

According to Corinne Heline, during the twelve holy days the Earth is enveloped with the love and light of the Cosmic Christ. The Radiant Christ makes four major contacts with the earth during the course of the year. These coincide with the equinoxes and solstices. The Archangelic Christ Spirit showers the earth with the rarest of perfumes. Every cell, atom, and molecule is infused with the love of God. This love permeates to the center of our planet and to our own Spirit. It becomes a wonderful time for soul dedication to the divine path of God.

The twelve holy days are the culmination of the four week season of advent which begins on the Sunday closest to November 30. Advent has been known as a time of purification and preparation for the holy Christmas mysteries. Early disciples of Christ believed this to be a time when they could receive inspiration from the other realms. The season of advent represents the steps on the initiatory path to become one with the Christ Spirit.

It has been an honor for me to participate in this very special time of year where the veil is lifted between the two worlds. These worlds are really one with angels, teachers, and the Christ, all awaiting our desire to know the truth of their existence. The concept of the Christ has been hidden in dogma and man's law. I believe the Christ to be part of the divine Trinity: Father, Son or Daughter (the Christ), and Holy Spirit Mother. The Christ is the "love of God made manifest." The Christ is not a person but an "office" or "position" we all attain to. I didn't say we were there, but aspiring to this. Jesus came to show us the way. He sacrificed himself to evolve the whole planet and each one of our souls. Why did He say, "You will do greater works than I" if the potential was not there?

In our busy lives, Christmas has become very commercial. We all have fun with gifts and celebrations. By participating in this ancient ritual of the twelve holy days, we can get back to what Christmas is really all about. It is a wonderful closure to the holiday season and will prepare us for the twelve months ahead. It will be a blessing to contribute to world prayer at one of the holiest times of the year.

As the old axiom says, "Thoughts are things. Energy follows thought." Entertain the possibility that our combined "thoughts" are co-creating with the Great Spirit, God Goddess, Universal Intelligence, Cosmic Consciousness, Allah, the "One." If enough of us live with peace in our own lives and see peace for our beautiful Mother Earth, maybe we can make it happen. Please, on these days and every day, pray for peace!

One year, on the ninth holy day, January 3, I was enjoying my daughter and grandsons at my home. All day long I kept telling them the thought meditation of the day: "Ye are the light of the world." (Matthew 5:14) I have one window in my bedroom where the sun shines in on a little table. I had a quartz crystal ball, cut flat on the bottom, sitting on a cloth. I was lying down relaxing and all of a sudden I looked over and saw smoke! The sun's rays from 93 million miles away came in my window and through the crystal to start a fire! It was a confirmation of what I had been saying all day, "Ye are the light of the world." Each one of us has a special light to shine and share with our planet. Be mindful of what you say!

Chapter one starts with the first holy day, December 26. Each subsequent chapter follows for each day. The meditations are to be read on the appropriate holy day. The reader can then explore his/her own messages and revelations.

Be aware each day of the disciple, sign of the zodiac, thought meditation, attainment, and spiritual center. When you sit or lie down to meditate, concentrate on the thought meditation for that day. See the spiritual center illumined in your own body.

As the days progress, see the previous spiritual centers illumined also, until the twelfth night when the whole body is seen in light.

These meditations are to be used for the Christmas season and also during the time the Earth travels through each sign of the Zodiac. For example, as we are in the sign of Aries, read the meditations for the holy day of Aries. The universal focus for that time is "Behold, I make all things new." (Rev. 21:5) The life and work of each disciple can be studied and used for inspiration. The book can also be opened any day at random to receive a message for that day.

The meditations I share with you came through me. The writing was effortless. I would light my candle, be still, and then the words would come to me.

These words are being shared in the hope that your hearts and minds will be balanced and open to the divine in all of us. God Goddess is within and everywhere present. The Spirit does speak in a "still small voice." We have to be quiet and start listening.

With love,
M.C.B.

Christmas Meditations on the Twelve Holy Days

December 26 - January 6

First Holy Day
December 26
Aries

"Behold, I Make All
Things New."
REV. 21:5

✑ Chapter One ✑

FIRST HOLY DAY: DECEMBER 26

ARIES: MARCH 20 - APRIL 21

DISCIPLE: JAMES - BROTHER OF JOHN

SPIRITUAL CENTER: HEAD (SEE ILLUMINED)

ATTAINMENT: TO SEE GOD IN ALL PEOPLE,
TIIINGS, AND CIRCUMSTANCE.

THOUGHT MEDITATION: "BEHOLD, I MAKE
ALL THINGS NEW." (REVELATION 21:5)

1981   In every aspect of the physical world there are positive and negative, and with God all things are possible. All things are renewed and taken up to the altar of life for new rebirth. Every aspect is used and used again. With the power of thought and mind, and through the grace and power of God, we can make all things new. We think and breathe that breath of life into our precious thoughts. We can rejuvenate and revitalize any situation or problem that may arise. We are one with the Lord. He hears our every prayer and invocation. We pray in faith and all is answered through His will working through us. In the name of Jesus Christ our prayers are answered according to God's will.

1982   To change a circumstance one must change his attitude. The eyes see what they want to

3

see. With the soul's capacity for understanding, we live according to our belief. If we behold a thing with light and love, it will forever be that way. If we see God in all things, our vision will always be clear and beautiful. With this God-given power of creation, we can change the world to a better place, where all know truth. We can all share in the responsibility of caring for one another. We give constant thanks that our Lord breathes every breath with us. As we think, we become. Every moment is a new beginning. Eternity is now. With life and love, every thought creates the next moment.

1983   In the mind all things are possible. We are given our own decisions to make things appear as they do. "Behold"- with that word we invoke what is to be. We set in motion our life around us. Our thoughts take shape and all comes into us as we see it. We think and behold a concept, then all of nature follows through. With our one mind together, we can create peace in the world, a new world of harmony and love where brother and sister love one another. By seeing God in all and everything, there will be heaven on Earth.

1985   The most disheartening situation can be changed using the power of the mind, the power of thought with God's energy. God makes all things new, new life, new hope, and new love. Behold it, see it, and it is there for you if asked for the benefit of all. Our lives are transformed when we ask with intentions of love. All things are made new, all disease is healed, and all hate is turned to love.

1986　　We are shown the way of creation with the day to day accomplishments or defeats. With our powers of the five senses, all originating in the head, we experience a small portion of the power of creation that comes from God. With our sight to behold and with our imagination, we see within the mind's eye what is needed. We picture it, then with our feeling and devotion, creation comes forth, but only if it is good for mankind.

All things are made new with the power that springs forth from the head. We imagine it and it comes forth new. "As a man thinketh in his heart so is he." (Proverbs 23:7) Our mind is linked with all minds. The one mind is the many. That power is linked with God's mind, as we are all one. That mind is God's mind because all is God. That enormous dormant power lies within each one of us. See it, hear it, taste it, smell it, touch it. It becomes new with God's power working in and through us. When we master life, the creation takes place immediately.

1991　　Behold - with my eyes I make all things new. With my ears I hear the divine music. My lips taste the sweetness of life. I smell the perfume of the most fragrant flowers permeating the very air we breathe. I touch the Earth and heaven with all these senses. They teach me of my world and yours. We are embodied to translate these feelings into wisdom for the soul plane. I speak and my words are filled with this wisdom. As the divine spark ignites, my life's true meaning is shown to me. It is all in a pattern. This small pattern of my life reflects countless eons of time, as my soul wandered from body to body to finally embrace the temple we call "home."

We listen to hear the angels speak to us. We can hear only what we want to hear. I can hear someone say that they love me, or I can hear them say that they damn me. With what I choose to hear, lessons come in. I can make life out of them or put them to sleep with unknowing. I meet someone and hope our paths can communicate. We see and are sometimes blind.

Give me the sight to know the truth. To be honest and verily so. Give me the eyes to capture Your essence, God, to light my way to You. Tasting the fruits of Your labor and mine, tasting the foods of Your knowledge, let me bring into my body Your essences, or more so, let Your seed grow within me, so that life becomes joy and the divine is so apparent that I see only You.

With the breath comes life - the ebb and flow. As I breathe, God's life comes into my temple. Let me breathe in the sweetness of life. Let me give forth the essence of light. May the in-breathing (the receiving) and the out-breathing (the giving) be equal in Your sight…as this life embodies Your will…as I touch with all of my senses…as my hands let me do good works for Thee. Let me be a handmaiden for You, Father Mother God, and be a true child who only loves.

1992   God's presence is always within us. As we think, we are exercising our God given power to create. Our thoughts take flight and are brought into reality of spirit. If we choose love, our world will be the beauteous planet that it can be. Its pure beauty reflects what we too can become. The healing waters flow to cleanse our planet and our being. Our tears wash away our sadness, transform it - "tears are excess blood." (Bishop Amy Johnson, D.D., Church of Tzaddi) Our tempers, as fire, burn out our seeming inequities with light, breaking all down to ashes to be reborn. The air, as mental mind, transforms the very ethers to obey our ideas.   The Earth, as Mother (matter), gives us the opportunity to live the physical life, where everyday challenges bring forth learning from heaven above. Each moment is a necessary part of eternity. We can change our whole destiny at this time, but will we?

1993   Try to see the bliss in the knowledge that God is in everything, every situation, and every atom of life. In so believing, all has a divine purpose for our higher learning. We are called to do our unique job on this Earth, to learn the many lessons in love. The Christ in us is that love which grows each time we bless instead of curse...each time we look with kindness and cooperation, instead of hate and damnation. We all have the great capacity to only love and heal ourselves and those we meet. Our lives, but dramas, are played for a higher purpose, for an understanding of the nature and laws of God the Father, God the Mother, God the Son or Daughter, whom we are growing to emulate.

Our job is to love and dream the perfect dream of happiness, brotherhood, agreement, plenty…a world where all our dreams for good come true…where each heart is blessed with the knowledge that God and man are one. When we can live in peace, our lives will follow. Trauma happens to awaken us to what is going wrong. It happens to show us our path must be altered. Trauma comes to force us to change…to beckon the good in our lives and souls to come forth. Dream it for good and "behold," all is made new.

1994 "I make all things bright and true. I am your life, your beloved. I am all that is and ever will be. I am the breath of your life, the heartbeat. I am the dream of your most wonderful dream. Try to use Me for good. Try to control your thoughts so that goodness and mercy will shine through. Be at one with Me as we create a new world of hope, love, and charity. Be as one with the Holy Father Mother God. Be with Me as we love the world, as we make the right decisions, as we both dream peace on Earth. We become one, one in spirit that is in all. This realization will bring heaven on Earth. The veil between the two worlds will be lifted, and all will see God as one with man.

"Dream of love and it will come. Dream of peace and it fulfills. Know I am always with you as we dream the new world into reality. Be at peace and know the 'I AM' of you is really you. The love we share, all the love you feel, comes from the heart of My heart. This spirit of love is universal and is always available. When we turn to love, we accomplish peace on Earth. Dream these wonderful dreams of brotherhood, sisterhood, and the establishment of fairness. No more war, as we truly begin to see that God is in all and is all. The very essence of your being is filled with light and no thing but God, the creator of all, the benefactor of all life in this material universe and in all universes.

"Try to remember, even in your fear, that My will is the supreme action of this universe. My will supercedes your little will. I am always working for good, regardless of the appearance. I know what is best, what is needed for your enfoldment, what is needed as necessary for your growth. Relax and know I guide your every step, as a mother does a child. For you are all My children and I only love you, love you forever, at every eternal moment of the blessed 'I AM.' Thank you for being My special children, the children of God. I am with you always until the beginning and end of all time. With Me all time is eternal, all life precious, every breath counted, every dream known, every moment of kindness remembered. Do know I care for you and wish the highest and best for you at every moment. You need everything that is happening to you, you need every moment of time to get to know Me…to let Me participate in your life as your loving parent. All love is yours as you begin to know I am forever in you as Love."

1996   The mind creates new and wondrous things. It has the capacity to shape and reshape entire lives. The head is the center of all the senses - the vehicles of self and the powers of emotion. The eyes take in and see what they want to see. They close when it is too much to bear.

The lips taste the sweetness or bitter medicine of life. The teeth break down and chew on ideas and thought. The mouth speaks words of encouragement or denial. The tongue wags or dances with light and praises. Words are spoken with love or foreboding. The ideas take shape with sound. The sounds create joy or disaster. The truth speaks or is hidden in dogma or lies. The silence encourages or damns its opponent. The trials are many - the praises infinite.

The ears hear love or the temptations of ego. The sound is a blanket of new fallen snow. The ears hear wisdom or the chatter of gossip. They hear the celestial music or the damning of children. What have our ears been privy to? Where does your angel go? What does she listen to? Is it joyful and God-praised or sickly and hurtful? With what we hear, our thoughts take shape. With who and what we see, our desires are known. With what we taste, our image can enliven or fall away in dust.

Our nose is the anchor, the sensory vehicle that

awakens our senses. Before we speak...before we see...the aroma of flowers can be at your feet...the stench of death can permeate your life.

To touch or feel is the emotion of love - it is a knowing without words - a dance without music. To be loved is a gift from within and above. To feel is to know the answer to questions. How do I "feel" about this decision or that? It becomes the barometer of life. Am I thrilled and happy to take this road or that? Does it make me happy or sad to choose this way or the other way?

With all of our senses our minds create form. With all of our joys, form takes shape. We imagine our blessings, and with all five senses our desires can manifest and bless our path. Many a dream has gone by and been forsaken. Many a wish has been trampled in soil. The wishes we make are to enrich all others. The choices we can make can change all of our lives. As one gets the understanding, the others will follow. Truth waits to be brought forth from the eons of soul. It awaits your asking; it answers your call.

1997 "The all is mind. The universe is mental." *(The Kabala)* We were all created as a divine spark in the mind of God. All of creation started in the mental planes, where the one universal force of love moved and all visible manifestation was formed. We were and are One. We started as one thought, lovingly cherished, lovingly fashioned out of the one universal substance...the one cohesive force of the

Cosmos – Love. God thought and we became the visible realms.

We have been chosen to participate in this great drama to begin to understand the reasons for all our deeds. Our expectations have become our creations. Our hearts move and matter takes shape. We are representations of the one creative force of the universe. Our lives have become out-workings of God's will on planet Earth. We have been chosen to incarnate at this time to bring the planet into its higher evolution - where angels walk openly with men…where love reigns…where the "law of allowing" makes room for a zillion ways of life… religious understanding… truths… actions… interests… joys. All become acceptable as different expressions of the one force - God. We have come here to emulate the differences, complexities, simplicities, beauties, likes, and dislikes of all there is in the universe. The one God really controls all. We are vehicles, expressions of that love. That love comes in many forms. "The wrath of God is love's severity."

We are here to have joy, be joy, and enjoy. Our lives are stages of development on the path to knowledge of truth. There are millions of truths in the universe. The first and last truth is that all is God - every person, plant, animal, air, fire, water, earth. All are God - every moment, action, reaction, love, hate. Truth is here, not in some distant far off place. Truth is here in your heart and mind. Bring the two together and there shall be eternal bliss.

1999   There is a time to start over, start afresh, and renew the old. The phoenix can rise out of the ashes. Dust can be formed into new life. Base metals can be put through the fire and come out pure gold.

It is time for our Earth and our bodies to rejuvenate, to start anew, recreate each cell to reflect the light of God…be filled with the awesome power of life, renewal, and creation. Each cell is a miniature sun that reflects God and all His wonders. This can be done as our bodies rebuild themselves every seven years. This can continue until we leave our Earth. Each cell has the potential of health, beauty, and renewal. Believe it can be done. Ask and it shall be given to you. Amen.

2001   Behold, the light has arrived on Earth as each one turns inward to see the truth of their being. The Earth is stepping up in vibration. The truth will be known. The messengers have arrived and are in place to spread the "good news." Our thoughts and love can transform this planet, can save it from destructive forces that some humans have called in. The truth will be known in every aspect of our lives. It will be shouted from the rooftops and the clouds. The Great Spirit wants love for this planet, as each one turns to peace within their lives. The reality of peace will prevail as the mighty hands of the divine hold our hearts in prayer.

2002   The Creator in us is our divine

birthright. It comes to us as our first gift. We are renewed each day as the "new" sun dawns. From our heavenly dream world, and our reconnection with Spirit, we are given respite to continue on in the daytime. Choices are given to us as we follow "the path" or swerve away from it. The Father Mother Creator is always working through us in love.

GOD, WHO AM I?

God, who am I?

One of the billion, trillion specks of love, Me, in the universe.

God, where am I going?

Back to Me, to love, hope, pray and create.

God, why am I here?

To learn love, be love, express joy, and create beauty.

God, why do You want me here?

To be an expression of Me in all My glory.

God, why have we fallen away from You?

You never did; it just appeared that way.

God, what is our future?

As all time co-exists, your futures are being created now.

My bet is on you kid, to be the best a child could be in expression of Father Mother God.

God, what can we do to bring the one thousand
   years of peace?
Look deep within and discover your true being.
The lights of the universe are reflected in your eyes.
Your hearts are made of the purest gold.
Your minds can create beauty, health, and love.
Balance the head and the heart,
Looking and seeing with heart, and
Loving with wisdom and understanding,
Knowing always that I LOVE YOU.

Second Holy Day
December 27
Taurus

"He That Dwelleth In Love,
Dwelleth In God."
JOHN 4:16

ᦸ Chapter Two ᦵ

SECOND HOLY DAY: DECEMBER 27

TAURUS: APRIL 21 - MAY 22

DISCIPLE: ANDREW

SPIRITUAL CENTER: THROAT
  (SEE ILLUMINED)

ATTAINMENT: TO BECOME A PERFECT
  CHANNEL OF GOD'S LOVE AND HARMONY.

THOUGHT MEDITATION: "HE THAT
  DWELLETH IN LOVE, DWELLETH IN GOD."
  (JOHN 4:16)

1980   God is love, and only love. He loves and creates. When we can become pure channels of His loving will and spirit, we dwelleth with God. He loves totally, no judgments, just a caring Father who wants only good for His children.

We are created out of God's love and are here to do His work. Our union will come about when we give up self for the whole, and beam out love for life and all in it. When we love, we lift up a part of us for reunion with our Creator. We realize that "I and my brother and sister are one, and I and my Father are one." When we feel a part of the whole, we can truly love and understand humanity. We desire to do God's work, through man, in love for all.

1982   Our body is the temple where the in-dwelling Christ spirit is alive and waiting to be born anew. Love is sent forth from our being through our heart and through our words. Words are power to our world. We speak and it is done. The holy sound transforms cosmic energy to physical substance. Know that He listens and speaks through us. The Christ child is born each time we express love to all. That love purifies and heals all who receive it. Love guards our door to the Lord, where all beauty and understanding can enter and dwell. We give thanks that all are blessed in His name.

1984   To dwell in love is to dwell within the Holy Spirit, where all grace is given unto thee. Loving is seeing divine order in every action, being able to accept all as God's will. Our hearts are linked to God when we love. His light shines through us. He wants us to love so His work can be shown here on Earth. Even the darkest moments can be eased and transformed by this power.

1986   Love is the purest emotion. It is the well from which all life springs forth. It is the prime mover of the universe. It binds one to another. Love contains within itself all emotion. It lives in our heart within the seed atom of perfection. It is that seed of perfect love that contains the infinite possibilities of the Christ Spirit, who came here to show us that perfect love.

When one loves, he reaches others by actions, but

mostly by the spoken word. Each word is never destroyed. Each sound we mutter is forever reverberating out to the cosmos. If those sounds are love, picture the heavenly vibrations that are never destroyed. Likewise, picture the negative words that can hurt and destroy.

God's love waits to spring forth as we meet people. One smile, one kind word is always remembered. One loving thought heals all.

1990 Dwelleth in love and all shall be given. Speak words of truth and all shall be tamed. Loving thoughts heal and enlighten. Caring thoughts enrich and enliven. Dreaming of the perfect world makes it come true. Hoping for a harmonious state of being brings it into reality. Wishing for and willing for perfection gives it the power to manifest.

God spoke forth "The Word," and creative fiat gave to man a golden throat to create form. As it is spoken, with God's power, words create. When we learn to give love and harmony in every thought, word, and deed, our voice becomes the lost creative word, the word by which all manifested creation comes forth.

I speak and my words are imbued with power. His thought, my word, His deed. His breath becomes my breath as we think and bring that thought into word. Creation is formed.

1991 Light comes from within. Darkness preceded the light. We must have one with the other.

Dwelling in one place supercedes the next. These are all manifestations of God. Our fore-fathers had a basic understanding of cosmic truth but missed one thing. Out of darkness comes light. We must know one to know the other. Our lives are but patterns of time that have been repeated over and over until we get it right, until we choose love instead of evil. God only loves, He does not damn. But the mighty laws of the universe do not let us get away with harming. Harm leads to repercussions. Love leads to more love. Evil creates more evil, as the mighty hand of retribution pays back.

Remember to love as our Creator has always instructed us....love as Jesus showed us. Through His suffering He was purged. Through His love He was cleansed and purified. Through His obedience the Lord of Hosts shone down on Him. The Christ lived in His being as He lived a totally loving life. God's goodness comes to us as we love. His graces forgive all failures.

1992   One day the power will be so great that the lost "Word" of the Bible spoken in the ethers will form that idea instantly in the physical. Through God's almighty power, our word will bring forth any necessity from universal substance. When ideas do not manifest, it is not the Father's will for us, not good for our higher learning. Our talents, when recognized, can open a floodgate of opportunity for this physical use. These talents are to be shared by all. Begin them now or wait an eternity.

1994   The throat will become the creative fiat by which all things shall be made. The Holy Spirit will operate through the body temple to bring all to your remembrance. Love will reign, and joy will replace all sorrows as God and man become one in Spirit, a oneness that will finally be understood and cherished instead of being feared and not believed. All men and women will take their rightful place. Peace will be on each one of our faces. Strife will end, and the beauty of the spiritual world will be opened to all humankind. We will know our place and our purpose as one with Father Mother God. Joy and peace will be the norm instead of the exception. We will work for the common good of all, each to establish Heaven on Earth. The profound will become the mundane as we are shown our many invisible helpers. Men and women will be looked upon as equal, knowing that contained within each soul are both the masculine and feminine attributes. Both are present in all and all is one.

The most important lesson we can learn is to accept all as being from the Father. He sends what we need and at the exact moment it is needed. "It is faith's work to see loving kindness out of the roughest strokes of God."

1996   Our Earth has a heartbeat that our hearts are linked up to. As the Earth beats her drum, we beat ours. What are we doing to save her? She is Mother to us, and as children what have we done? What expression have we learned and what duties have we neglected? It is our responsibility to bring light and anchor it into her many sad places. She has supported us and how have we paid her back? Do we bite the hand that feeds us? Do we poison her soil and create havoc? With her incredible balance of nature, how have we treated ourselves? With love? With destruction? With hate? Regrets? Joys?

Now is the time to change our path. Earth is calling to us as a mother does to a child. She is a divine exquisite creation and we have been given stewardship over her shores. How can we change things? Who is responsible? Everyone must start where they are. Treat people with love, and friends grow around you like beautiful gardens. Think before you act. Listen to your heart - it speaks of love. There is a way to heal the Earth and her people: Believe that every moment is God filled and directed…that the Earth is an extension of us. Our hearts and minds together can create the perfect garden she used to be… snake and all. The snake is wisdom; she comes to teach us, not to kill. Let our eyes be opened to the possibilities of humankind. Begin with love and all will follow.

OUR EARTH

Our planet is dying.
Don't you hear her cry?
Her beauteous rivers and valleys,
Choking with the waste of man.
Her once pristine water, clarity, healing,
Has gone by the way of industry.
The air so alive, the breath which gives life,
Is choking with chemicals and smoke.
The waste that will last for a million years,
Cannot find a resting place.
Don't you hear her crying?
This beautiful life.
Does she not reflect what
We are doing to ourselves?
Our bodies, the decay, the abuse.
The terror, the fear.
Stifling the Spirit.
The I AM that I AM,
GOD IS, SO WE ARE.

1997   "My dwelling place is love. Its home is the heart. It reaches to all corners of the universe and comes right back to live in you. It deems the impossible. It sanctifies the improbable. It performs the miraculous. It feeds all souls. My love encompasses every atom of space - it soars in between the atoms of quantum theory. It fuels all sources of energy. It lives in each breath. It creates anew at each second. My love forgives all weaknesses, all harmful ways. It understands the fall from Spirit with compassion.

"My love knows no boundaries yet is in all the limits of time and space. It fills the entire cosmos and creates more love. This love can be yours, yours for the asking.

"It can fill your being at each moment of time. Like the eagle, it can lift up the most downtrodden heart. It can sing like the sweet birds in the morning welcoming the new sun's light.

"The past is over. The future is what you make it. The now is when I love you, filling your spirit to encompass the whole world. This love is possible to create Heaven on Earth. Its life lives each moment in the creation of time. If I were to speak, there would be words of love…love…evolve. Love evolves into more love. All is in divine order with helping unseen hands. Every moment counts as My children grow into beings of light where love dwells, heals all, is all. Amen."

1999   The Earth is about to leap in evolution. Our very cells are changing to magnify God in His holy temple. The possibilities of humankind are endless. All can be healthy, happy, and wise. It is our divine birthright as the wheel of karma comes to an end... a stop, shift, and start up again into a higher evolution. God's love redeems all ills of the past. It is time to be reborn in the light of love, so that all may know that the Spirit loves them equally, no matter what they do.

2000 Every creation of God is wrapped in love. We are created and exist in this love. Every action of the universe contains the law and essence of Spirit. We understand our truths according to our development. It is time to accept every moment, every action, every minute wave of fire, air, earth, and water as directly from the movement of the Creator's love. All happens according to the divine plan with every experience necessary for our higher learning. We are here to express the Divine. That is our sole mission. The great "I AM," the great "One," moves and breathes and we have our life. The awareness of love in every breath will be known.

2002 This is a loving world. God has given us all things necessary for the perfect life. We are here to create joy. All else is a path leading to destruction. We have been given the tools for peace and prosperity. The physical world has many temptations leading to joy. It must be joy for all, not just for ourselves. Our striving leads to sickness, our surrender to unlimited bounty. Why is it that some people succeed? Success in the world view may be utter failure in the "Law of

Right." Bounty must be shared, and it must be given with an open heart. This produces the great life lived with love and compassion, available to all.

2003 God is the one supreme power, the one cause and effect of all workings of the universe. The Lord reaps and sows every seed of thought, word, and deed. The One Power is in control of all the workings of this planet and all the stars. Once we accept this, magic comes into our lives. We accept all as coming from the blessed hands of the unseen. We know all to be the right workings for our evolution. We see all as right action and justice. We know that every experience is for our highest good. Trust "the process of life." The "flow" of the river leads us to our divine destination. All is known in the end to be directly from Universal Substance. The Great Spirit loves and adores us just the way we are.

Third Holy Day
December 28
Gemini

"Be Still And Know That
I Am God."
PSALM 46:10

๑ Chapter Three ๑

THIRD HOLY DAY: DECEMBER 28

GEMINI: MAY 22 - JUNE 22

DISCIPLE: THOMAS

SPIRITUAL CENTER: HANDS
  (SEE ILLUMINED)

ATTAINMENT: VISUALIZE THE HANDS AS
  CENTERS OF HEALING, PEACE, AND
  WISDOM.

THOUGHT MEDITATION: "BE STILL, AND
  KNOW THAT I AM GOD." (PSALM 46:10)

1981   In the stillness we find strength.   In the quiet we find refuge. From that place comes the only life that gives us breath and our being We are here for understanding. We translate and transmute our understanding of God.

In the silence the Lord speaks, not always in words, but in light and love. "I AM" declares that the Divine presence is within. "I AM" lives and loves and has its being within. Silence speaks, hearts listen.

1982   The source of all life and power is within us, the spark of infinity that grows as we express more of the Christ Child of Love to all people. Our hands do God's work through peace and under- standing. Our hands are extensions of the heart that can express beauty to our world. Instead of running

29

and searching, look within. There we find creation, love, and the power of God the Father and Goddess the Mother.

HANDS

Heaven, cloudy, clear horizon.
Hands holding our heads and hearts,
Hands that show caring, healing,
Life and love.
Communication from your heart
Tells how you feel.
Listen. "The Touch Speaks."
As the eyes can see, so can the hands.
The hands of God become
The instruments of His will.

"See! I will not forget you…I have carved you on the palm of My hand." (Isaiah 49:15)

1984   Be still and know the Lord is within you. Be still and see truth from the depths of your soul. Be still and listen. Watch and you will see miracles of faith come to reality. We run, we search, we never stop thinking. In the moment we are finally still, we will hear and know that the good Lord abides in us. Forever eternally, "I AM that I AM."

1985   Being still helps us to perceive the Divine. We are so used to observing the outside world that we forget to be quiet and listen for God's breath. The world is just one manifestation of the many creations of the "One." Going to the opposite end of this brings us to the experience of God as the "still small voice." This part of our Creator is virtually unexplored on our planet and in our current evolution. It will become our saving grace in the years to come. We will draw upon the power within, the very life that perpetuates this physical form.

The stillness is Spirit, the opposite end of the hustle bustle of our world, the one end of the positive-negative pole that goes from Spirit to matter. Silence on one end, sound on the other. Matter becomes Spirit Eternal.

1986 Each time we say "I AM," we create an energy that heals and, by its very nature, creates what we say next. Every time we say "I AM," the power of God surfaces.

All creation starts in the stillness. "There are no words in heaven." Words are not needed there. They are only a tool for living in the physical world. In stillness is all movement. From the stillness comes all action. In that quiet of space, we can hear the OM, the I AM of God, which brings all material into manifestation.

WORDS

There are no words in heaven.
But look what words do here.
They come to bless us, come to haunt us;
Come to love us, and to damn us.
Words, some chosen with thought.
Others fly out with unexpected swiftness.
Words can calm the most tormented soul.
Words that one mind can touch with another.
Some words bring with them the joy of the
morning.
Others close the day with darkness and
foreboding.
Which ones will come out of my mouth?
Ones that come from the heart?
Ones that will become as blessings on wings;
That bring love and happiness
And, one day, wisdom.

1989   I and the Father are One. We breathe the same breath. We think the same thought. Our going out and our coming in are resplendent to His nature. We are One. We live in each other. As He lives in me, my existence is through Him. His thought creates my being. His dreams make my dreams real. His body embodies my body to function in this world and the next. His beauty is within me as a small reflection of His great power. His truth can be known, if I am still.

1991   Profound peace comes over me in the stillness. My life becomes a tool, a channel of Divine life force, an empty vessel which yearns to be full. The lesser me tries to take over and grasp all the material things it can. The greater me fills my soul and waits for Divine expression. The stillness brings strength, the very challenge of God's energy bursting in my veins. Living in each breath of wonder, peace envelopes me, and I know that I and the Father are One. I am here because the Great Spirit wants it that way, for the expression of my soul's life force. Here I sit in the stillness and wait upon the Lord. His life gives me life. His love sustains me as a child of God.

1992   As we open the door of acceptance, we can encompass great beings of light, Spirit helpers, who surround us and come to our aid. They come to help us when we ask their assistance. The angel assigned to us never leaves our side, and entwines us with love and devotion, as we transform our own being into an angel of light. The angels will protect us from harm if it is God's will. When calamity strikes, it is for our higher learning. Our dreams and minds create these situations for our highest good. We have exactly what we need at every moment of our lives. We are told what is needed from the higher realms and agree to take these hardships on. Our lives become an ever upward path of devotion to the second coming of Master Jesus and Mother Mary. The second coming will also be in every one of our hearts and minds.

1993   Be still and listen, and what do you hear? The breath, the life, the essence of good cheer. The being of creativity beckons you to go deeper and unite with the Creator. We are all unique living parts that make up the whole of the "One Spirit." The Father lives through us as we become more in tune with His will. His will can become our total life, where everything we touch and everyone we meet are blessed. The Holy Spirit Mother brings all gifts to us of wisdom, truth, healing, and beauty. If we obey His/Her law, our lives become as perfect flowers, blooming each day. Awake, arise, and blossom as the Christ Spirit of Love becomes our true identity.

"Be still and know that the I AM in you is really the I AM in all. All is one life, one Spirit, one magnificent essence linking all together. We are all part of one another in Spirit. The I AM of each one is the I AM of Me. I give you life, hope, and the energy for any power that transpires. Every cell, every breath, every moment is directed by Me. My body is in your body. My soul is in your soul as love, light, will, and power."

1994   "I think and the universe is created. I will and all transpires for good. All is in divine order...all, in perfect love. All is a necessary part of life as you learn to reach the very Spirit within. Every movement is directed by Me. I love and all takes shape and form. All is in Me and I AM in all.

"My life is the essence of creative thought. All I think comes into being. All I AM materializes from

Spirit. Spirit is behind all material possessions. I give all to those who love Me, those who follow My will with grace instead of fighting. Surrender to Me, child, as I show you the I AM of who you are. I cradle My child in the arms of the universe. My arms and hands encompass all. I live in you with a peace that only I can give, a peace only I can manifest. Fall into My arms, My mind, My lap. Let Me guide, carry, and work with you for the perfect good. Let Me guide you to My innermost secret place which is in the very depths of you. It is in the center and life of you and all.

"Be at peace while I love you eternally with joy and direction. I will carry you to the place of contentment, where all appearances are accepted as My will, where all seeming evil is seen as the necessary part of the good.

"My hands are in all and directing all. There is not one moment not guarded by My will of love and right action. Be at peace as I fill you with My love, fill you with such joy that you will be aware of Me only. I love you, child, rest with Me."

1996   The moment of creation started in silence. It began when the heart of God opened and loved. It began with the first breath of the universe. The first thought created the beautiful forms we see. The first sound uttered brought the physical into manifestation.

From the void there is all and nothing. God spoke and all was formed by His word.

The silence holds the key to unlocking all secrets. In the stillness, man creates his own life.

It is time for humankind to lift their consciousness...to ask why...why are we here? What is this glorious game all about? Why has my soul chosen to be here at this time? The still small voice speaks from a place of silence. The "voice" is your very own part of God...your speck of infinite time and space. This spark ignites when you begin to go within- all answers and directions to your life are there. Your guidance is ever present as the living Father Mother within.

The need for divine direction will be very important as we enter the next dimension...as we travel where most of us have not gone before. The Starship Earth is about to enter her greatest adventure, her grandest leap in evolution, as one day experiences as ten. Each twenty four hours will be equal to a mini lifetime of changes. Our perceptions and guidance is ever growing. Every little step has meaning. All is for the grand drama about to take place. Fasten your seat belts for the Triple EEE Ride of a lifetime. The Triple E of Eternity as we see it begin right now.

1997   The forces of nature prove the existence of our One God... every plant, animal, rock, and the Earth... all in beautiful symmetry and equilibrium. Man stepped in and altered that balance with his selfish ways. All this for a "higher evolution?" God will overcome.

We are one with the Spirit of life. The breath transforms death into life. Each breath goes through every function of our bodies. One breath of wind in the sky never dies, and lives on. One ripple of the sea affects the all. One sound echoes through our so called time. Time is an invention of man. It delineates what we do, how we live. In Spirit's universe the all is right now. This moment contains all of the past and all of the future.

It is recommended that we live in the moment. We are told to "be here now." Why? Because this is the moment of creation. Our thoughts make our world right now.

The attitudes of the past and the hopes or fears for the future can all be changed in an instant. Our whole destiny can be transformed by one breath...one movement of air...a fallen leaf...a turn of the head... a smile to a stranger.

The Lord is ever present for the "knock at the door." He waits patiently for that one miraculous moment when we become "Self - Realized." That moment can alter future generations of our own family and the whole family of man. That instant of truth where we understand that Spirit made us and never left us alone. S/HE created our souls, our spirits, and our bodies to live eternally in the oneness. The truth awaits our call.

Are You really there, God? Are You deep inside of me and all around me? Have You not created everything I see and all of the unseen? Are Your miracles of life everywhere present? Is Your hope of eternal life possible for me? Do You love me like Your child? Is it time for me to grow up? Grow into the mystery of life itself...the understanding of our oneness...the possibility of me hearing Your whispers and being the love that You are? Is it time to mature, to take my place as representative of You on this Earth...to fulfill my divine mission...to express the love I feel in my heart? Is it time to take my wings, soar like the eagle, to be fearless? Is it time to step up to the situations facing me every day with grace, acceptance, and understanding...to look at my trials as being Your mighty will in action...to accept whatever comes to me in the appearance of good or evil? Your Will works through every human, animal, plant, and mineral.

There is the possibility that, truly, all is love. All appearances are You in action. All is within Your allegiance. All is the One Power acting for the benefit of all. Could this be the hidden truth? Even in the Bible it is stated, "God creates the good and the evil. He creates the light and the darkness." (Ezekiel 32: 8)

Matter has become the duality, the seeming separation of all life forms. This separation is an illusion. As Yogananda said, "Maya is illusion - the measurer...the magical power in creation by which limitations and divisions are apparently present in the immeasurable and inseparable."

Look at the innocence of a child and remember who you are. In the stillness of your room, recall the truth. "Be still and know that the I AM of Me is the I AM of you." The I AM denotes God's life in you and me. Remember?

1998   It is our birthright to know who we truly are, where we came from, and who we will become. The Holy of Holies can be reached on a mountaintop, in a cave in the high elevations, and also wherever we are. This sacred place is right within our heart, closer than hand or foot. The Great Spirit remembers each one of our joys and sorrows and "takes the chaff from the wheat and with the breath of kindness blows the chaff away."

"A friend is one whom one may pour out the contents of one's heart – chaff and grain. Knowing that gentle hands will take and sift it, keep what is worth keeping, and with the breath of kindness, blow the rest away" (Arabian Proverb)

2000   Listen, for the angels will speak to you in your sleeping dreams and in your waking dreams. There are always clues along the way - signposts to help you to the next step, your next level of awareness.

It seems that sometimes we are lost and downtrodden. Nothing seems to be going our way (the ego's way). Our way is not always the best experience for us at that time. It is always a "just" experience, but somehow we don't see it that way.

The ups and downs, the duality, shows us the way back to the one even keel. When we serve, we are "in the flow." We accept what is happening to us in our "boat" (Noah's Ark). (In a dream I looked down and my two shoes were two Noah's Arks.) With easy waves, Noah's Ark is in our very own shoes. It is our very own way to salvation, being saved. It is our task to accept and create for the good. I AM speaks at every moment. Be still and know.

2001 There will be a time of no secrets, where truth will reign, where the wonders will never cease, where love is law and, as law, obeyed. The wise ones will triumph. The sad souls, greedy for so called "power," will be whisked away to a planet where they can play their deadly games. The "One Life" will flourish on our Mother Earth, and she will shine with her beauty and splendor. The truth will prevail. Peace will prevail.

2002 In the stillness we hear the workings of the 27,000 billion cells of our human/divine bodies. Each atom is a universe. Each cell is a whirling conviction of the Creator's energy. All are moving toward harmony or chaos. Our bodies are the Temple, the center of the cosmos, the spark of humanity and divinity rolled into one powerhouse of the life force.

2003 "Be still and know that I AM your Creator. Know that peace is possible in this sometimes tumultuous world. Be still and know that

I AM TRUTH. I AM the one power of the universe for good. I AM the one truth of your existence. Be still and know that I AM LOVE, the love you feel in your hearts and minds...the love that transforms all to the good. Be still and realize your divine existence, the possibility of peace on Earth, the reality that I guide every action of this planet, and beyond. Be still and know that I love you, and know that this love can heal the world and bring the Millennium of Peace."

Fourth Holy Day
December 29
Cancer

"But If We Walk In The Light,
As He Is In The Light,
We Have Fellowship One With Another."
JOHN 1:7

৩ Chapter Four ৬

FOURTH HOLY DAY: DECEMBER 29

CANCER: JUNE 22 - JULY 23

DISCIPLE: BARTHOLOMEW

SPIRITUAL CENTER: SOLAR PLEXUS
  (SEE ILLUMINED)

ATTAINMENT: TRANSFORMATION IS LEVELS
  OF UNDERSTANDING - THE SOUL REVEALS
  THE TRUTH.

THOUGHT MEDITATION: "BUT IF WE WALK
  IN THE LIGHT, AS HE IS IN THE LIGHT, WE
  HAVE FELLOWSHIP ONE WITH ANOTHER."
  (JOHN 1:7)

1980   When we walk in the light, we walk in love. The perfect love sent forth is like the sun that helps everyone and everything to grow. The Christ light of love shines for those who can open their hearts and have "fellowship one with the other." We "live" according to the love we can share.

1986   Within the soul is all our past experience, all the eons of time we have existed. All truth and understanding are within the infinite soul of our being. They wait to be brought forth. All this memory is here for our education. As we walk in the way of Spirit, more is revealed to us.

Our physical sun is symbolic of the Universal Spirit, the Life Force. We are all connected to the sun with a shaft of sunlight. This ray comes from our sun and unites with the son/daughter of the Spirit within. It is as if we move around our world encircled in a pillar of light, linking us with the sun (Universal Spirit) and the sun of our solar plexus, our soul. These many pillars of light are all linked together in a matrix of energy, quite like a crystalline structure. The crystal signifies man's potential of energies, which can be directed or received according to the need. As we unite with Spirit, this pillar of light is strengthened. It becomes a protective shield that directs and guides us.

1991 Beware, the times are changing. No longer can we get away with evil for any period of time. It will come back on us much sooner. Karma never dies, but sometimes it takes a while to return. It will return with the swiftness of a sword, striking down the evil in its path. Every day is a judgment day, and all evil must be transformed to good. Our Earth is alive and wants to stay that way. Beware of those who try to kill her. The laws of nature will turn the tides as everything is in divine order.

1992 Jesus came to show us the way, the way of the perfect son or daughter of God, the way to the truth, the path of discipleship where each man or woman becomes the Christ, which is the "love of God made manifest."

1994 We are now repaying our debts and

our debtors. We are making up for the inequities we have committed in all of our lives. When the wheel of Karma is balanced, we will no longer learn through suffering. We will learn through love.

1996   Walking in the light means walking in love. It is a knowing of the continuity of all life forms, a trusting in all processes of evolution. It is an understanding that God's will is supreme and that all happens for the best.

The fear of death will be abolished. It will be known as a changing of form to higher realms and vibrations. People will move from one dimension to the next, the eternal moment of "no time," "no space." No time, where all time, past, present, and future, is happening simultaneously. No space, where everything is instantly where we are.

How can we doubt the truth with the miracles we see everyday: the beauty of nature, the efficiency of our glorious physical bodies, the moment of birth. The essence of life beckons from within. All people we meet are gifts for our learning, treasures much richer than gold.

Life can be known through the journey within. No other person can do this work for us. Hundreds of teachers have come and gone. Volumes of beautiful words have been written for guidance. The one true guide is the Holy presence within. Truth speaks from the depths of your soul. Be patient and kind with yourself and others. The light will shine in the darkest hour.

45

1997   The soul is the record of all Earth and other planetary incarnations. It is our subconscious mind that is like the computer chip, recording all our experience. At each moment we have within all the necessary tools for enlightenment. For each task, a different quality is tested, a test of reason or the heart. Each circumstance is a revealer of truth, where we stand on the understanding of various spiritual virtues. Our hearts are examined to see how much we can love a situation or person. We are constantly tried on our knowledge of Universal Law, our willingness to cooperate with others, and our readiness to stay on "the path."

When we are confused or uneasy, it is a signal that something is not right, that we are going against our soul's mission to truth. Each experience and every word that is seen or heard are all signposts on the way to making a million right decisions.

When we are in the "flow," Spirit carries us up and down through life's experience. It is our divine mission to accept all as coming from the One Source.

It is our ego self that fights the "flow" and points the finger at outer causes for our dilemma. The power begins in you and me. It starts in our thoughts and gains momentum through our emotions. The passion we feel for what we want creates anew. The imagination shapes and fuels our desires to be born only if they are for our highest learning at that moment.

Be still and realize that the God you seek is right

within your bones. The mighty I AM presence is one with your Spirit. That part of you is eternal, immortal, and ageless.

Are we helpless pawns in a mass hysteria of delusion, or are we in fact powerful beings of light caught in material form? Have we not chosen to be here during the most exciting and frightening time of our Gaia-Earth? Hold on to your hats, it might be a bumpy ride. Chaos! Do we have to have all of it? Or is it just a shaking up, drowning out, firing up, spewing out, blowing apart, or freezing up of all that is dead, unkind, false, unrealistic, and trying?

There are two options. All of this means nothing, or, every mini second of time is God centered, God directed, and God loved. It has been written, "And I saw a new Heaven and a new Earth. For the first Heaven and first Earth had passed away." (Rev. 21:1) "As above, so below." (Hermes, Thoth) Remember in the seeming confusion there is Divine Order. Be not afraid. Fear not.

1999 Fellowship leads to family among friends. We are destined to make our friends our family. Everyone we meet, in potentiality, is linked to us on a soul level. In gratitude we thank God for all our friends.

It is time to cast away prejudice, to accept and embrace the uniqueness of each individual or group. All are on their own path leading back to the Spirit within. It is time to put down our weapons and instead bring tools of trade to work together for the common good. Our Earth is a wise Mother. She will not let us down if we will respect and care for her. Nature, her mighty fury, is only cleaning up what we have let go astray. The destruction we see is a reflection of what goes on inside the collective consciousness. Be the beauty and serenity of Nature and it will reflect in your outer world.

2000   Look at the suffering of Jesus, what He had to endure. This will not be necessary with our total union. We are graduating because of His work. All the great saints and masters have come to show us that there is no death, only "eternity to spend with those we love."

2001   The vision of peace starts in our hearts. The outpouring of God's life force will bring peace to this planet. As each one chooses peace in his life, those around will be touched and want the same for themselves.

It is time to stop and listen to our hearts. Can we truly live in the "peace that passeth all understanding"? (Philippians 4:7)   Is it time to evolve and sing a different tune on our Mother Earth? The time is near when the final choice will be made: to live in fear, destruction, and turmoil or turn within to the glories of our eternal Spirit. It is the time to choose, making peace or creating war. Which one to choose…which one to choose?

RUNNING

Running, running, but to where?
Meet one here. Meet more there.
Scurrying to find happiness.
Racing to capture fulfillment.
Leaping to consume.
Searching for what's good tomorrow.
Maybe if I keep running,
I won't have to think about me…
Who I really am,
What I really feel about life,
Where I am going.
This glorious race leads us back to
Just me sitting here.
Loving the world or hating it.
Making peace or creating war.
Just me alone.
But tied to trillions and zillions of other stars.

2002   It is our duty and gift to give and receive love. Jesus' greatest knowledge to us was to love one another as He loved us. Even in His darkest hour, He looked at His betrayers with compassion. He saw their faults and forgave them, "For they know not what they do." As others hurt us, maybe they too have no idea how painful it is to us. Kindness can be the healing balm for all hurts. "Do not resemble those who injure you." Love yourself and all else follows.

HURTS

Sigh or cry it out.
It doesn't belong there.
Deep in your heart lies
The sadness of past hurts,
Broken dreams, unfulfilled promises.
Let them go, as a wave goes out to sea
And then is born again anew.
These hurts can be given back...
Given back to God, back to Mother Earth.
All blessings come when we empty ourselves
Of all frivolous things,
Knowing that our being expresses
The very Heart of God.

2003 "Trust in Me. I will lead you to a new life. I will model what is needed to bring balance and harmony to you and yours. Trust your own instincts, not someone else's. It will unfold before you. Trust your own heart, and it will open to new opportunities. It will lead you to your hopes and joys. Believe the answers are within you. Believe I will guide you to your destiny. Believe I will show you the way - the way of the heart and mind balanced. Trust once again in your gut feeling. The emotions are a key to learning and knowing the way. Trust Me again, when all else fails. I AM within you as Love."

Fifth Holy Day
December 30
Leo

"Love Is The Fulfilling
Of The Law."
ROMANS 13:10

∽ Chapter Five ∾

FIFTH HOLY DAY: DECEMBER 30

LEO: JULY 23 - AUGUST 24

DISCIPLE: JUDAS

SPIRITUAL CENTER: HEART
  (SEE ILLUMINED)

ATTAINMENT: LOVE TRANSFORMS OUR
  LIVES AND GIVES US THE POWER TO "PUT
  OFF THE OLD MAN AND PUT ON THE NEW."

THOUGHT MEDITATION: "LOVE IS THE
  FULFILLING OF THE LAW." (ROMANS 13:10)

1980   On Earth and in Heaven, there is one law and that is LOVE. If we love totally, we become the Christ. It is the one link that brings us together. When love shines forth, it transforms everything it comes in contact with. Love heals and regenerates. When love is present, all else is comforted.

1981   Love guides and directs every action of God. Our Universe reels on this one power. Every action of our world brings with it the attitude of Divine Love. All other conditions are but the negative pole of the one positive force. When we love, we invite the harmony and beauty of the Earth and Heavens into our path.

1982   Love is the attraction and cohesive power of the Universe...the cord that binds. Every atom is held together with this law of attraction. Life force or

"Chi" is Spirit's energy in action. God's thought becomes the eons of time.

All action comes from this power of love. It transforms the lowliest of creatures to the highest of Heaven. It creates and generates more love, making new each one it touches.

By our trials, we see that the way to salvation is to "Love thy neighbor as thyself" (Matthew 22:39) because one is part of the other. Without each one of us, the Universe would not be complete.

When perfect love reigns, the Golden Age will arrive, bringing with it glory to God's Heaven. Our destiny is to experience Heaven on Earth. We are children of the Lord, waiting for the presence of each Higher Self to emerge.

1987 To "Put off the old man..." has to do with patterns of insecurities, selfishness, old ways of thinking, and restrictions either put on us or that we have adopted through ignorance. The "new man" is one of love. Loving is an understanding of the law.

Within our body temple is the possibility of unimaginable blessings and benedictions. If we love, we rejuvenate every cell. His promise of peace and health manifests. Acting only in love creates a new image and likeness of the Spirit within.

1990 Let me love You, Lord, as You love me. Let me love myself as You have shown me Your love. Let the world be embraced with the truth of Your existence. Let every atom shout forth its love and unity. Let all living things know how they are connected in oneness. Let the dream of the unified world in peace transform our hearts and minds. Let Your love, for an instant of eternity, be known to all. Let us share, at that moment, Your wisdom and truth. Let the sun so shine that our hearts match that light. Let our hearts fulfill the law, knowing that God and I are one, You and I are one, one in Spirit, no separation, only God's love made manifest.

1991   Love yourself as no one has loved you. You must accept yourself as God accepts you. His love is mighty, strong, unwavering. His love is all encompassing. He loves only, no matter what you do. As you sin and hide further from His light, He beckons you to return. He understands our faults, our darkest deeds.

The so called "bad events" are but reflections of our lack of love. They are reminders that we have not obeyed the law, that we have transgressed it. Our hearts can be opened with prayer and sacrifice. Our hearts stay open when we choose love.

Every action is written, every thought is remembered in the ethers (The Akashic Record). Every thought of love creates more love. Every thought of hate propels more hate. The seed of perfection is within us, waiting to blossom and grow.

1992 I pray that each atom, molecule, and cell of my body is filled with love. I pray that at any moment I can express the love that is now within me. I pray that every human being and living creature be filled with this joy and light.

Every living thing is imbued with the Christ Spirit of Love. This one thought, multiplied, will transform our planet. It will elevate its aura of love to be as brilliant as our sun, but in a different way, almost a reflection of the sun.

The sun's double will be seen in the heavens as Mother Goddess takes Her divine place in the Trinity. I have seen two suns, one above the other, in brilliant light. Our Father Mother God awaits our return to total union with the will, love, and wisdom of our Divine Creator. Matter is transmuted into Spirit and Spirit back into matter. Spirit whispers in every breath: inhale – receiving (feminine), exhale – giving (masculine). Somewhere in between we are alive in the Christ love.

TWO SUNS

Two suns represent our Father Mother God.
Shining in our heavens they will show us
The balance of the positive and negative.
Our Father Mother teaches us
The strength of union,
To produce the perfect Son or Daughter of God –
The Christ, the presence of love in our universe.
These two suns will shine when we produce
The balance of this planet…

When woman takes her equal place with man,
When God is seen as Mother as well as Father.
The sun giving life, growth, and light represents
The love of the Cosmos.
When Mother God takes Her place with Father God
In our hearts and minds,
The two suns will be seen by all.

1993   Love comes in many forms. The actions we perceive as punishments are really Spirit showing us how to love. All that transpires in our lives comes from the one source. All that we encounter is for our own good. Every situation, every temptation, every trial is directly from the hands of the Father. There is only one power, God's power. It is man's choice to use it for good or evil. Even the seeming evil is a necessary part of our learning. Only in the physical do we see the duality. In reality there is no action of any human being that does not have the dominion of the mighty will of God behind it.

1994   Our lives are blessed as we maintain the "flow," accept all for our higher learning, accept all as the will of Spirit. Our problems begin when we choose to fight and resist what is happening. If we surrender to the flow of God, the flow of good in the universe, we will have peace.

We can heal our greatest difficulty by acceptance

and by surrendering to God's will, to "what's happening." We can sometimes take action to change it, but if it doesn't work, then know that it is necessary for that time. Spirit gives us lessons we need in many different forms. Some may bring us joy and life, and others may make us tremble with fear and death.

Even Judas had his perfect place in God's plan. Without the "villain," and the death of Christ, there would have been no resurrection. Even Judas had his place in the divine plan.

1996   Love heals all wounds. It is the great sovereign balm of all worries and torments. It can change the darkest day into a bright sunshine filled wonder. When we love, we are in tune with our Creator. We sing the song that creates more love and harmony of the planets. As we love, a tone of music goes out from us. It blends with the heart sounds of those we love. They feel it working wonders in their soul. All these sounds together create the celestial "Music of the Spheres."

To love means blending with others in a melody of song and praise. It can move the tallest mountain and the tiniest ant. Be aware of your thoughts of love. As you send them out, they ricochet right back to you.

LOVING THOUGHTS

Wings of caring love;
Thoughts sent out with fire;
To blaze the trail for the reality.
Loving thoughts have that special flight.
Their fire beams like the sun.
Christ's love beams that way, too.
Forever this energy reveals
How God's work
Manifests itself through you.

1997　　Be at peace and know that no matter the appearance of calamity, disruption, and chaos, there is love behind every action of this world. There is a reason for suffering.

It has become the only way to learn our soul lessons. There is coming a time when we will learn our lessons through love. This has always been our choice; but in our dilemma, in our selfishness, we have chosen the hard way. We have chosen to fight the tide, to battle the wave of the flow of God. Do we fight something for a thousand years, a lifetime, fifty years, one day, or one moment? Can we accept what's happening to us as coming from the mighty hands of Spirit?

When life doesn't go "our" way, we try again and find that the outcome may be delayed or never manifested. These circumstances become necessary blocks to learn something new or experience something we never dreamed of. The unexpected result is the best one; after all, everything happens for the best. In the end, looking back, the outcome is always for our highest option, always the greatest gift.

We have all these lessons and all these lifetimes. What is it all about? What do we need to get it right? There is one simple answer to the most profound question of the Cosmos. After eons of time, centuries of living, thousands of bodies, zillions of breaths taken, what do we have to do to get it right? LOVE!

Love yourself, love others, and accept people for their beautiful differences. There are as many paths to God as there are people. No one's path is 100% right, but it is right for that person. Allow freedom of thought. Allow people their unique expression of love and devotion to God. One may choose a cathedral of stained glass and marble. Another may choose a cathedral of the open sky and mountains. Celebrate all choices, especially when they don't hurt anyone else. Keep your beliefs close to your heart, and in your heart you may say, "I am right." As *A Course in Miracles* says, "Would you rather be right, or happy?"

Allow everyone their level of understanding of the world and God's relationship to man. Allow people to thrive in their phases of life and understand that all men and women are expressions of the One Source. Give up the old and make room for the new. Peace begins with you.

SEE ME

See me for who I am.
Look into my eyes and my heart and
Really see me.
I invite you to know me,
To be a friend.
With my faults and blessings,
I look to you,
Not for what group you belong to,
Not for the color of your skin,
Not for all your beliefs in God and man.
But I look to you
For who you are.
Look to me
For who we both can become.

1998   Let us step up to the challenge to love all and be wise in our reactions to each other. Let us be reverent to our own lives and the lives of others. In our respect and honor of all the Kingdoms of Earth - human, animal, plant, mineral - let our dreams of peace manifest now!

1999   "Death, where is thy sting?" (I Cor. 15:55) For that one moment of death, one second when we are not sure, one breath leads to the other world.

61

DONNA FRANCESCA

Death is just an open door,
The soul's journey to eternity.
Heaven can be there.
Love abundant, freedom.
Rejoice, the Spirit lives on.
Wings of fire, wind strong,
Light up the pathway,
Color, sound, remembering,
The beginning of time.
Tears and laughter.
God bless her journey.

Sixth Holy Day
December 31
Virgo

"But He That Is Greatest Among You Shall Be Your Servant."
MATTHEW 23:11

◦೨ Chapter Six ◦ఴ

SIXTH HOLY DAY: DECEMBER 31

VIRGO: AUGUST 24 - SEPTEMBER 23

DISCIPLE: JAMES - BROTHER OF JUDE & SIMON

SPIRITUAL CENTER: INTESTINAL TRACT
(SEE ILLUMINED)

ATTAINMENT: AS WE LOVE, WE ARE
PURIFIED...THIS LEADS TO SERVICE.

THOUGHT MEDITATION: "BUT HE THAT IS
GREATEST AMONG YOU SHALL BE YOUR
SERVANT." (MATTHEW 23:11)

1980   When   you   love,   you   become
purified...this leads to service.   Why service?   To
enlighten.   When we serve, we are treating the other
person as ourselves. We are looking at them as a child
of God, a part of God.   When we serve man, we serve
God. He created us all to be equal. He put a part of
Himself into all of us. He lives in each being. We live
because of Him.

1981   When we serve, the angels help our
many paths.   There is an unending supply of energy
when we work with the Lord.   He guides our every
step. He watches and His will works through us.

We travel many roads, but the way to service is the
giving of oneself to others to help them along the
path. When we give, we receive. When we love, our
light shines. We see others as ourselves.   When one

65

serves, each one is blessed. Our hearts are open to the ever abundant supply of love and light.

1982   Trial and error are the only paths to understanding. The more correct decisions we make, the closer we come to the Christ presence. All experience is a necessary step into the Kingdom, which is our natural state. We serve to express the love that the Lord has for each one of His children, loving equally and with compassion, seeing all and knowing all as one in our Father's name.

1984   When I serve, I serve God. When I help, I fulfill the Law of Love. Love and service are God's tools for us, His tools to find Him. His love comes through to those we touch. Our prayers are answered when we look to help all those in need. There is always one more unfortunate than I. Reach out. There is always someone to care for.

1986   As people see the selflessness in service, they are given an example to emulate. The greatest souls will reach out to help the lowliest, because they know the truth of the divine being in each one of us. When we serve our fellowmen, one by one their hearts are healed, and they remember the kindness and pass it on.

1987   Service is the highest gift we can give each other, knowing that the mighty "I AM" Presence is within. This serving acknowledges His presence and qualifies as a gift from Spirit. It is our ceaseless job to help all those along the path. We are expected to help until every soul is lifted up.

1991   Our spirits are frozen in this time and space. We have come to make this physical world as perfect as the spirit world is. The divine pattern extends from Heaven to Earth. The consequence of this is separation. Our goal is to unite Heaven with Earth.

Jesus came to show us that the Christ Spirit can rest within a human being. The Christ presence of love is the perfected son or daughter of God. His presence can abide in a soul who has purified itself enough to welcome the growth of the Christ within. Through His many lifetimes, Jesus perfected His soul to welcome the Christ Spirit. His personality stepped aside and the power, love, and wisdom of God worked through Him. He became one with the head and the heart of the Christ forevermore.

1992   Serving is a gift we give another. It is the glory and attitude of God made manifest. It is a mother's duty and position in its natural state, a sublimation of one's own desires to serve another. As a child is nurtured and grows, his mother lays aside her desires and gives to the child. It can be done in balance, and in its proper order, is a gift from the universe.

MAMA

Mama, Mama, look to me
And see all that you will.
See me with arms open,
Heart alive.
See me look up to you and
Watch out for you, too.
Here I am small, but my
Spirit is of the universe,
My soul my very own.
My heart belongs to the world.
Make the world for me a loving, caring place
So that I may do the same for my children.

It is the giving of gifts that brings us closer to God. We can try to leave something out, but it is always brought into balance with the intention to serve. The angels complete whatever gift we may give in service, and it is never forgotten.

Our lives can be a healing tool to those we meet. Our little triumphs add up: a smile, a kind word, a loving glance, a touch of the hand. All can be of service as we learn to give love freely. We are here to bring all of humanity together, to establish the fact that we are all one in Spirit and that our lives are intertwined. Every act of each human being affects the whole. The answer to the quest for the Holy Grail is, "How can I help you? What can I do for you?"

1993   Serving brings us closer to the will of Spirit. It is hoping the best for everyone. It is wishing that all lives are blessed. It is the Father's desire to "Give us the keys to the Kingdom." It is His will that we have all the gifts of Heaven, peace, health, wisdom, and prosperity, so that we may spread that love to all. There is an "outpouring of unlimited life force" that is available to everyone (Jin Shin Jyutsu® #10).   Look around; there is an unending supply of bounty.

1994   When we become closer to Spirit, we want to help, enliven, and give hope. Each one has a gift to give.   For some it may be on a grand scale, helping thousands of people. Some may help in small ways every day.   One kind word, one helpful action, can change a whole day.   Sometimes it can change a whole life.

All is at peace, as I pray: Our Father Mother, know me as I hope to know You. Teach me Your ways, show me Your love. Let me be Thy love to everyone I meet.   Let me become the light that gives life.   Let me pray and love You more every day. Let the "little me" give way to the God of me so that all of Your Holy works can be given out through me.   Let me show Your peace and healing to everyone. Let me serve You as I serve my fellowman.   Let my heart and mind be pure in the way that the Christ, Your perfect child, is pure.   Let me be a flowering of Your love.   Let me be the peace I wish for the world and be the love that I know You have for me.   Let me become one with You, one with the Christ, and one with the Holy Spirit. Let all know that God, man, and woman are one, and that all peace is possible as we unite forever with You. Amen.

1995 Jesus came as the greatest Master. His mission was to help, heal, and serve. He was constantly trying to uplift everyone He met and to teach them the truth of their being. He wanted them to know His personal relationship with God as Father. He wanted them to see the possibilities of humankind. His mission of love was to teach how love heals all wounds, how faith in our Father Mother God can move mountains, how we are to respect one another no matter one's station in life, no matter one's past or present deeds. He came to show us the way of love through service. He was constantly serving all He met…a cup of water for one…a healing balm for another…a touch of His robe. Every meeting was for the benefit of others.

1996 As our oneness in Spirit is revealed, we will understand that by serving one another, we are really giving to ourselves. An act of kindness goes a long way. One moment of love lives on in eternity. A dream of hope creates a heaven on Earth. A moment of peace can last a lifetime. One smile can live on in someone's heart. Sweet words are like nectar caressing the soul. They are always remembered. So are angry words.

As each day passes, try to help someone in need,

by a touch of the hand, carrying a heavy load, loving words. Remember that as we treat others, we will be treated. As we judge, we will be judged. As we love, the same will be brought to us in love.

1997 Service is a way to lift up humanity to its next evolution. We have been there before in our journey to Earth. The cosmic fire was lit when Jesus took embodiment and became the Christ. He came as the way-shower for all people. His mission in life was to show us what all men and women can do when they dedicate their lives to love and service.

We have all been here many times, some more than others. Everyone tries their own way to enlightenment. One way is not better than the next. One way is not necessarily "higher" than the other. All have their places in the soul experience of each individual. Each person is sent to Earth to learn certain lessons. We come in with our "wish list" of what we are here to accomplish. As each wish is checked off, the next one comes to the surface. As our lessons are learned, another star, feather, or jewel appears in our cap. We are here to get it right. Either we do it right now or we wait until the next time.

We come into each life with the necessary tools for mastery. It is our choices along the way that determine the outcome. Our lives are connected with those people who need our lessons too. A parent who cannot love may teach a child to love themselves unconditionally. Some souls just do not have the stamina to

71

stay on the "right road." They become selfish and self centered, caring nothing about others.

The perfect life is possible when we give up part of ourselves for the good of all. The Master always has a moment to converse with the student, even if it is only one sentence uttered. When our lives can be given up for service, we know we are on the path to becoming a Christed soul. Many lifetimes of preparation are needed to begin this process.

Once you set your foot on the spiritual path, there is no turning back. It becomes your greatest desire to glimpse the truth of our existence and to understand even one minute part of how this miraculous universe works. The quest for knowledge becomes the focus of your life. This great giant puzzle and its pieces seem to begin to fit together.

There is a reason behind every action of our universe. When you understand this, the smallest inconsequential exchange takes on new meaning. Your spiritual journey begins to be lived for each moment's sake, the "now." The journey's end becomes another vista of exploration and deliverance.

All this leads us to is the quiet of ourselves and all the reasons we are here at this moment. This passage has us alive, alert, and present at one of the most exciting times of our history. We and Mother Earth are about to graduate into the next dimension where the veils are lifted, and Heaven is seen where it has always been, right here on Earth.

Believe it to be, and it will be. Our combined thoughts and prayers will create how we arrive in the next dimension. The whole answer is attitude. Do we see the world in chaos, or can we trust and know that everything that is happening is for our highest good in spite of appearances? God knows what She is doing. Remember to see peace, to see our Earth in harmony, to dream the dream. Then it can be the reality. See all life living in peace among nations, freedom for all to pursue their understanding of God Goddess. It is a blessing to be born into this Earth family at such a time. Give thanks and hold on to your hats. It's going to be a glorious ride!

1998   Let me be the handmaiden that Your Mother exemplifies…Mother Mary, who emulates the highest feminine Deity. Her example of purity and acceptance is a beacon for all. She watched You die to be resurrected. She accepted all as from the hand of the Father. Her Spirit never wavered from the one Spirit's will working in all conditions. Her pure heart and mind shall lead us on. The feminine polarity will be united with the Patriarch. The Matriarch will once again take Her place as equal. Women are the vehicles for life in this world. We are to be respected as the feminine expression of God.

Mother Mary, help us to love like You do, and cover us with Your mantle of protection. As You keep Your ever watchful eyes on our beloved planet, light the path to You and Yours. Open our hearts, as Your immaculate heart prays. Thank You for being the Queen of Peace, and the Queen of the Angels. Show us Your love so that we may do the same for others. Amen.

WOMAN

You are the opening into this world
From the mysterious light beyond.
You transport the soul
From its Spirit home
To its creation.
You are the handiwork of God Goddess
And Her miracles.
Her divine light gives you breath.
His mighty power gives you the gift of life.
His dreams for you are of perfection.
As Mary's pure thought and deed
Helped to create the Christ Child.
That power is within woman,
To be there when life bursts forth,
When creation brings into this life another soul
On its journey to the perfect life.
We begin as Spirit and Soul.
We are given choices of
Love and perfection or
Hate and damnation.
Which one to choose?
Which one to choose?

1999   She who follows God's Will can surmount all obstacles. She who sees love out of every action of the Universe can know the heart of God. She who knows the best for the situation will come out on top. She who sees the will of the Father in every action will know her heart's desire. She who treasures the tiniest seed will know the flower and fruit of her labors. She who sees God's loving kindness in all challenges can know the truth.

The world is truly run on love, the one power that pervades even the smallest shift of sand. The Father presides in all hearts and minds. He permits the evil men do to enable their higher learning. "Without a foe, a soldier never knows his strength." (*The Aquarian Gospel of Jesus the Christ*) Realize this great secret and all will be given to you. Know that you and the Father Mother are one.

2000   It is time to forgive and let go of the past. It is time to rejoice, knowing that the Great Spirit blesses all and guides our hands to do His work. It is our work to follow our own divine inner guidance that shows us the way to truth, the truth of the moment.

It is time to feel love for ourselves, and those around, to choose joy and the "blessing way." Each day we have a new chance to be kind and to walk in the footprints of the Master. Our lives are great opportunities to live the perfect life, to not falter in the path of adversity, to hold fast to the divine truths of who we really are…representatives of God Goddess in this physical world. We are all here for lessons in love. Believe!

2001 Trust in the Lord. The Great Spirit will provide all your needs. Trust His mighty hands to work with your hands to give you all that is needed for your highest good. Fret not, worry no more. It will be given to His children. Stop the push and rush. Live each day with grace, knowing that you are "covered." Stop the crying and hours of worry. It will be wise to put faith in the Lord. Know that He hears your every plea. Plea no more. Pray and give thanks as if it has already been received. Think of it as healed, and it will be written for you in the book of life. Peace child, behold!

2002 Joy is the remedy of life. It is our divine birthright to be joy and express joy. All the illusions of the past will be forgiven. The heart expresses happiness when there is harmony, a balance of the ebb and flow of life. Like the tides of the sea, the energy we give can be equal to the energy we receive. This is the love principle in action. It is the function of the spiritual "heart seed atom" that is placed behind our physical heart. This "atom" is the sum total of all the love we have experienced in our soul's journey. As we love, joy grows and becomes a way of life. Love leads to joy!

2003 You are chosen to experience more of

the other side of the veil when you accept the divinity
of our souls. It is time to join with those on the other
side and welcome the splendor of the unseen worlds.
Ask your angels and guides to help you, go before
you, and lead you to truth. Angels and guides
intervene only when asked. The heaven world waits
for us to acknowledge its existence, waits in the breath
of an angel's wing, waits to be known as the peace of
the world.

Seventh Holy Day
January 1
Libra

"Ye Shall Know The Truth,
And The Truth
Shall Make You Free."
JOHN 8:32

∽ Chapter Seven ∽

SEVENTH HOLY DAY: JANUARY 1

LIBRA: SEPTEMBER 23 - OCTOBER 24

DISCIPLE: ST. JUDE

SPIRITUAL CENTER: ADRENAL GLANDS
(SEE ILLUMINED)

ATTAINMENT: TO EXPRESS THE DIVINE
ATTRIBUTES AS A DEVOTEE AND TO SEE
BEAUTY IN ALL THINGS.

THOUGHT MEDITATION: "YE SHALL KNOW
THE TRUTH, AND THE TRUTH SHALL
MAKE YOU FREE." (JOHN 8:32)

1982   God favors all creation equally. His love knows no limits or boundaries. He cares for His Spirit man/woman equally and with no judgment. He delivers His will through every individual and every living creation on this planet and in our universe. His word becomes our word through thought and speech. We become co-creators. Energy lives forever, to be used again in different forms. God loves us and wants only the perfection in which He created us. There is only One Will. Maybe our "free will" is demonstrated in how we react to what's happening. ("Is God's Will What's Happening?") Do we accept the hand of Spirit in every action of our lives, or do we fight "the flow" at every turn, sometimes fighting for a whole lifetime?

We live to understand the workings of the Lord and to accept and cherish every breath we are permitted to take. Freedom comes when we accept all. God's will is always working through us.

IS GOD'S WILL WHAT'S HAPPENING?

God's will is what's happening,
Happening at every moment.
Only One Will, as Father Mother God
Uses us for heavenly work.
All in divine order,
Our lives unfold.
Free will is our reaction to the Lord's plan.
Do we choose to love it, or hate it?
Is it my will or Thy Will? Truly only One Will.
Surrendering means accepting all
As sent from above.

1983   When the adrenal glands are fully active, they provide the necessary power for any physical feat. They are symbolic of the greatest strength and courage that any person can have. They are the helpers, promoting enough energy to accomplish what is needed. They transform the idea into powerful action. If we had faith and knew the truth, then all things would be possible. God wants to give us the Kingdom and use us to cleanse the world. He wants us to be set free in love.

1986   The truth of God's nature in man will set

us free from the cycles of birth and death. The truth will lead us to eternal life and eternal consciousness. When we embody, we temporarily forget our true Spirit nature. When we know the truth of God's reality, we will see that heaven and earth are one and the same, just different degrees of the one life.

1987 As I walk I see "The Many Faces of God," each one having the divine spark of infinite wisdom, each one having the life that makes all things possible. Each person possesses the capacity for infinite love and understanding, is a perfect reflection of Spirit, has the seed of the Christ that is waiting to be born, has the potential to be the perfect son or daughter of God, and has the love of the Father written in his soul.

We take on these physical bodies, and their hardships, to learn lessons of the soul. Here we are severely tested…sometimes to win, sometimes to fail…but never really failing, because every experience is a necessary part of our evolution. All steps are vital for our understanding, each one a lesson to purify our souls.

1988 The truth is that this body is but a temporary home of Spirit. The Life Spirit within connects us to every other living being on this planet and in all other universes. Our Spirit is connected to all as we express the Divine Unity of "The One." Our time here is but a moment in eternity. Our lives are the testing ground of heaven and hell. We become what we desire to become. Our desires keep us here on earth. God's eternity is awaiting us on the other side of this veil. His perfect expression will be revealed to us at death. This truth will free us from all human bondage. It will free our bodies and souls, knowing this is only the temporary home.

1990   The truth is that every minute and every tiny speck of the Universe has the God force within it. We have our life through His being. Every action and reaction has the mark of Spirit. Our breaths and "our tears are counted and contained." (Eileen George, Meet the Father Ministry) Every moment is blessed. Every circumstance is an act of "The One Will," even the negative ones. Every evil somehow brings on the good. Our trials are hurdles to leap over, to get one step closer to our Creator.

1992   We express what is in our hearts and souls. We learn from our trials to choose truth. The basic truth is Love. Our tribulations are created by our higher self, the God part of us, according to natural law. We must experience everything that is happening to us. We all have exactly what we need at all times.

The power to do good is within us. The power to do evil dwells there, too. The Devil is of our own making. Yes, there is evil and it does gather force, but the power of God supercedes any evil. The Devil is within. It is the darkness of our soul. It is our own nemesis. Evil is the breeder of catastrophe, the destroyer. But it is necessary until we learn the divine truth that, in spirit we are all one...only in the physical do we have the duality of good and evil. "I can't believe evil can overcome the good." (Hallae)

God wants only good for us. The lessons of suffering are to leave with the Piscean Age, the Age of Separation. The glorious Aquarian Age to come will bring peace, joy, love, health, and perfected heaven on earth. Think it, believe it, see it, and as the moving mind thinks...SO BE IT.

1994   We are here to perfect our behavior and correspondence to the actions of other people. When we have learned all our lessons, our bodies become the home for the Christ Spirit...the perfect son or daughter of Love. Each one of us is on that mission every time we come to earth. We are given a great drama to unfold the many soul lessons we need to experience. We are here for trial and error. In Spirit we are constantly blessed with right action because the law works perfectly. On earth we are co-creators with Spirit. We are given the power to create or destroy. Herein lies the lesson of time and space.

1995   The mighty hands of the unseen overlook all that is happening. They go before us to lead the way. All experience is accounted for and taken as lessons in learning to accept God's will. We can go with the flow or we can fight it. We can love it or hate it, accept it or destroy it, claim it or shun it, trust it or be deceived by it, envy it or throw it away. Whatever happens to us comes for a reason. It comes so that we may more fully understand the workings of Spirit and so that we may learn to accept all as a necessary part of the whole.

Our lives are but moments within the choices we make for how life is to be. Our lives are like a book, with tidy pages well spent, or endless hours of fretting.

We can have it all! The very power of the entire universe lies within, awaiting our call, awaiting our love to grow, awaiting our minds to open and see, hear, touch, smell, and taste the divinity in us and in all.

1996 God is in everyone, even the mean, critical, obscene person. God is behind each life, bridging it to grow. We may judge and say that cannot be God. But if God is all, then does He not permit everything in the universe, even every "evil" deed? To know the light, you have to have touched the darkness. To know glory, you must have suffered. To know peace you must have known war. To love you have to have hated. Everything with its opposite is the lesson we have to learn. We must travail the depths to get to the heights. What in one man's eye you deem a blight may just be "a scar."

"Judge not; the workings of his brain and of his heart thou canst not see; what looks to thy dim eyes a stain, in God's pure light may only be a scar, brought from some well-won field, where thou wouldst only faint and yield." (Adelaide A. Procter)

1997 Our lives are interwoven with those who need our words and deeds. We are placed exactly where our highest learning is, right where it is needed. The truth is that God's law of love is always working through us, no matter the appearance. Our egos take on "power plays" that are needed for our evolution. A seeming cruel, harsh decision becomes a blessing in disguise. On ego levels, people are hurt and lives shattered, to only later be born again in a newness not dreamed of. In the midst of this hurt, hearts and emotions are all working together for the good.

Trust in the process with all its surprises. They will eventually guide you to the exact place God wants you to be. The depths precede the heights. When we neither swing too high, nor too low, our lives will become more balanced. When our emotions are more in harmony, more on an even keel, we will be sailing through life as if on a breezy sea. Work for the good, and all will be given to those who believe.

1998 Our lives are unfolding at rapid rate. Our lessons are manifesting faster and faster. The law of karma is speeding up, and the payback is much faster. No longer can man be able to get away with injuring others without the truth surfacing much faster. Lies cannot be told; truth will prevail. Truth will be unleashed. No more dark corners of deception. The "information highway" is symbolic and a literal expression of this reality. No one can hide from the truth. When we hurt each other or the planet, we will have the payback much sooner. All karma is being evened out, as the Libra balance of scales comes into justice.

Each cell of Mother Earth and each cell of our bodies are being transformed and awakened to the divine light that is inherent within. All the upheaval that we see in our world is indicative of what is going on in each one of us. We are here to face our maker, our mistakes, darkness, selfishness, and egotism. We are here to balance good and evil and to look at these dualistic ideas as all necessary for our higher learning. When our lives are in harmony, we will learn through love and joy. Our suffering will be finished for a time, as we express the universal attributes of Spirit. Our planet will once again be the shining globe of light spinning through space.

The arrogant, greedy, power hungry people of the world will also have to face their Creator. Those who destroy will be destroyed. Those who hate will feel that same hate. Those who deliberately take food away and try to kill this earth will be punished.

Our words will become all powerful, and in an instant the harm wished on someone else will boomerang right back onto the sender. The love will come back in that same instant. Which will you choose?

Our brothers and sisters are truly us. The human family is a family of One Spirit. Choose where your minds will be, and there your hearts will follow. Look for the unity of head and heart: masculine logic and reason coupled with feminine compassion and love. Woman will take her rightful place next to man. The qualities of love and compassion will come to the forefront to save this planet.

The world is literally in our hands. What will we do now? Pollute and poison her or nurture and clean up what we have done? The greed has to stop! The fast buck will be buried in the trembling cities. Be watchful of what you do, how you think, where your hands are working. Are they working for the good, or do they participate in the destruction?

THE BOTTOM LINE

The bottom line will do anything
To get what it wants.
It will pollute our rivers and
Damage our minds.
It will cheat and steal legally,
Not caring where is the next buck.
It will lie and represent anything to
Make those numbers roll.
Roll up only.
And if on the way down
It will kill off or fire,
That unlucky sap that stands on the bottom line.
What is this thing?
A pot that can only grow,
Or heads will spin.
What price riches?
Destruction of our glorious planet.
Defilement of our once – pristine minds.
Where can we run from those bottom lines?

We can heal this world. We can begin by healing ourselves. Others will follow the example. It is time to give up fighting and to start realizing that some people are just sick, sad souls, not knowing the process of life. Be at peace, and know that the Great Spirit is cheering for each one of us to fulfill our mission. Each one has a mission to love enough to save the Earth from destruction.

Are you destroying yourself with a long held anger, a desire for revenge, or a hurt buried deep in your soul? Are you punishing yourself for your own actions, or for belief systems placed on you from someone else that have translated into an unloving attitude toward self? Forgive the attacker. Forgive yourself. Feel the anger, feel the pain, and then LET IT GO! If you do not know how to forgive, hand this over to the Great Spirit and ask to be filled with divine forgiveness. It eventually comes.

The time is now. The hour is upon us. Have compassion, as all of us are in the same boat. Find peace within and the whole planet will be that peace. Ask for help from your angels, unseen guides, Spirit, your mighty "I AM" presence. "Ask and Ye shall receive." Spirit moves when we ask. The "still small voice" speaks in the silence. Now is the moment to listen.

2000 The dream of peace is within. It is carried to those around you. The ripple becomes the mighty wave. The droplet becomes the ocean. The tiniest seed transforms into the tree of life. This tree is within us, waiting to grow. The clouds are seeded, and water drops as rain. The rain brings the mysterious rainbow. The colors reflect the greatness of each ray of light. We are truly blessed at every moment. God Goddess watches all!

RAINBOWS

Each ray of sunlight shows us the rainbow.
When our Lord promised us a rainbow,
He left hidden that all light from our sun
Comes to us in all colors of the spectrum,
Making it certain
That all places on earth
Are the ends of rainbows.

"All know that the drop merges into the ocean, but few know that the ocean merges into the drop."
(Kabir 1450-1518)

2002 Freedom is our birthright, as representatives of the Divine One Spirit on Earth. Freedom is a state of mind. It is time to put away the shackles of fear. It has been a long held false belief that we are prisoners here. We are actually the "light of the world," waiting to shine forth. We are also the love of the world, ready to express beauty. It is time for us all to step up to our divinity…the Spirit of God within.

2003 "We have our plans, and then there's God." (Margie Battles, my mother.) We have all that is necessary for faith to enliven. We plan, we search, we prepare. Then all of our plans go awry. It is our planning that sometimes shows us ego and not the Divine Will. Timing is everything. If it is right for us, it happens. If it doesn't happen, it might come along in a better form, when we are ready for its completion. Do your work. Then the Will of Heaven will transform, and all will be for the good.

Eighth Holy Day
January 2
Scorpio

"Blessed Are The Pure In Heart
For They Shall See God."
MATTHEW 5:8

⊸ Chapter Eight ⊶

EIGHTH HOLY DAY: JANUARY 2

SCORPIO: OCTOBER 24 - NOVEMBER 23

DISCIPLE: ST. JOHN

SPIRITUAL CENTER: REPRODUCTIVE
CENTER (SEE ILLUMINED)

ATTAINMENT: THE ABILITY TO TRANSMUTE
MATTER INTO SPIRIT THAT HE NEVER
KNOW DEATH. TO LEARN TO HAVE
COMPASSION WITH ALL LIFE.

THOUGHT MEDITATION: "BLESSED ARE THE
PURE IN HEART FOR THEY SHALL SEE
GOD." (MATTHEW 5:8)

1982   The "pure in heart" bear witness to the
Christ in all. They see God represented everywhere,
in every breath of the universe. The mystic marriage
between head and heart is in balance. Many tears and
washings have filtered through the essence of the
heart. It blossoms like a flower, growing larger and
purer, unfolding as each kind deed is presented. The
petals open to expand the perfume of pure love. Our
thoughts work together with the Christ Love to bring
forth harmony and symmetry. The purest white light
channels through to bring joy and wisdom to
everyone who participates in the exchange. The heart
is like a fountain, forever giving and replenishing.

1985   When we love, there is perfection. Each physical atom filled with Divine Love can transform matter into Spirit. Each atom returns to its original substance…Holy Spirit. Love is the magnet that binds one to the other. It can transmute all other emotions to those of peace. Those who love will come to know Source. It is the way to get back to center. "Wherever I am, I am in the center of the Cosmos." (Mary Burmeister - Jin Shin Jyutsu®)

1986   Love me as I love myself. Love you as I love. Care for me as I care for you. Open yourself so that we may meet in the oneness of Spirit, in divine union. In infinite oneness we meet. In divine love, one becomes the other.

1991   How I wish that my heart was pure, so pure that I could see and know God, pure with giving and receiving, pure in spirit and bliss, pure in light, hope, and charity. I would always be giving out love, always responding with joy and gratitude. Being a pillar of strength and courage, a temple of insurmountable heights (open ceiling, where the clouds seep in), I would have an open pathway, straight to Source.

Here we live, but here is also the dream. It all seems so real, but it is only fleeting moments trailed into one time. In the whole scope of God's divine plan, our lives are only an instant, a twinkle of time. As we go through death's door, it will be "Oh yes, I remember this," with a feeling of rest, unity, no pain, only love.

PROBLEMS

There is this feeling of freedom,
Of a release of woes on this earth.
When perplexed with the different
Ensuing dramas of this life;
When looked upon from the higher picture,
Are but stepping stones and stumbling blocks
That must be glossed over.
This freedom comes from the realization
That in the mighty scheme of Heaven,
These problems are not real.
They are not as life-threatening as expected.
Nor do these problems last in our eternity.
They are fleeting like this life.
And in Heaven our spirits work out all
*   problems*
In connection with God.

1992   Matter is spirit vibrating at a slower rate. When we transmute matter into spirit, billions of cells become filled with light. Each cell brims with its greatest potential, spirit moving in divine order and love. As we control our thoughts, we can transform our physical body to Spirit.

We can learn to become like a child, growing each moment with the awe and joy of a new day. We would look at life with expectation, hope, and love with an innocent wonder, each moment precious, no moment forgotten, all a gift from The Lord God.

All the billions of stars rest in our own being. Our bodies reflect, and contain, the cosmos. Look to see the glory in nature and in each one of our faces. Know there is divine order in all.

1993   The world is in an eternal embrace. Each moment is so alive that all time ceases. There is a sweet smell of flowers in bloom with each breath. God cares for and creates every detail of even the tiniest flower. He watches the crawl of an ant, compared to the force of an erupting volcano. The lightning brings veins of light from God's body to the earth, rejuvenating the "life force" or "Chi" of our planet. He is the billowy white clouds of a blue afternoon, the gray foreboding clouds just before a storm, and the brilliance of spring as life blooms in perfect time for the renewal of earth.

Become still, listen, and dream of the earth in peace, in the garden where we began. These moments of contentment can still be felt, even with all of life's troubles. In the quiet, we can feel close to our Creator. Looking within, we see the vastness of space. We can know and receive the will and power of the Father, the truth and wisdom of the Mother (Holy Spirit), and the ever present love of the Christ. Open your eyes to see the ever expanding creations of Spirit.

1994   "Nothing happens without My dominion. All that transpires is really My will. There is one power, one God Goddess. Man uses it for good or evil. The one power is always present. Man chooses to hurt and wrong, but it is still My will that is everywhere present, all knowing and all powerful.

"Your lesson is to love always. Love your earthly mother and father, even if they do not love. Forgive, and know that your Heavenly Mother and Father know the best for you at all times. I am waiting for your love so that we may embrace as one. Love, no matter the circumstance, no matter the "enemy." All are lessons from Me."

1995   Your life is but a drama of eons of time all encompassed in this great eternal "now." Just think, in "reality" there is no time or space. All life is simultaneous this very instant. All you have ever been, all you are now, and all you will be in the future, is alive right now. The potentialities of this moment are only infinity. All are alive. There is no death. If there is no space, then the Universe is right where you are. All those you have ever loved are alive at this moment, perhaps in other forms. Their spirits are eternal. They still love you as you love them.

1997   To limit the limitless in our body temple is a miraculous phenomena. As we reach out in our astral bodies (emotional bodies) in dreamtime at night, we see we can even fly. Think of someone or something, and it is right here. Think of an object and it manifests. The astral body brings us our desires, lets us feel the essence of those things we choose to have in our lives. The astral body feels the pain. That is why sometimes we feel "spaced out." During great pain and great joy, we actually lift out of our bodies. At these times it is just too much to take.

All is moving energy. All cells are minute universes in action. Every breath goes through every function of the body. We are tiny replicas of the Great Cosmos. Everything we need for healing is within our body temple. Every cell is really spirit vibrating at a slower speed. When the body's "life force" goes below a certain frequency, pain and disease begin to manifest. When Chi is restored, the body then has the ability to heal itself.

Each cell of the material world can be transmuted into Spirit. This is how Jesus took His body with Him. Every atom of His physical being was transmuted by spiritual light to become Spirit. His "temple" became the perfect "wedding garment" to wed the Christ Spirit and become part of the Trinity. Our lives can take this path as we endeavor to emulate His life of love.

1998 To be pure in heart is to choose love. It is a sweetness, a child-like view of the world. We come to the knee of our Father Mother God and obey like a child.

There are infinite expressions of the one Spirit. We are all put here to live our unique pattern. Honor your path and the path of others. Trust that the good Lord will provide for your way. As the birds and trees are all cared for, the tiniest ant is counted. We too are looked after by our Heavenly Parents. We are chosen to express the One Spirit in our own beautiful way. The temptation is to exclude those whom we may judge as not worthy of love. The evil we see men and women do, the trials that people put each other through, the hatred, guilt, and sorrow individuals feel for themselves, all these must be acknowledged as part of our higher learning. We are truly "stuck with ourselves" for eternity. So we might as well accept who we are and learn to modify our behavior.

This waking state, called "awake," is one minute aspect of what is really going on in our soul. There are apparently millions of layers of consciousness and dimensions we function in. Every expression we use, every thought we think, every object we see, every sound that comes into our ears, all have a reason for being.

We redeem our works, at the end of our lives. How was each meeting with another soul - was it with compassion and love, or careless and unwanted? All these events are counted on the scheme of time. These occurrences are woven into our tapestry. Are they of fine silk and orderly, or is the pattern chaotic?

When you look at someone or something and can truly say, "I am that. I am that," then the oneness has manifested in your life. Ask to be shown the way, then look, listen, and contemplate the smallest sign. God can be loud and boisterous like lightning and claps of thunder, or He may speak to you in the gentlest whisper, saying, "Love Me as I love you."

1999 Thank you Father Mother God for all Your gifts of Spirit. Let me use these gifts for heavenly deeds, ones that will make You proud parents of successful children. We can do this! It takes one life to change the world. If enough people "get it," we all get it. Let's do it NOW!

2000 I had a dream this afternoon and woke up to people singing about mercy. "In man's consciousness there appears so much mercy, so much love, that these have been called time and space." (Edgar Cayce 3660-1) There is so much mercy in the world that it cannot be counted or measured. In the place of no time, instant manifestation is a reality. Time is collapsing, and past, present, and future are all conscious in the great eternal NOW. We will know what it is like to be instant creators. As the need arises, it will be given, if it is the Holy Will. God's grace and mercy abound and fill every atom of space. Time and space are an illusion of this world, a way to see separation and division. In Spirit all is one and the same, with all knowing the truth.

2001 Dreams of peace will bring it to fruition. The belief that the majority of people on this planet are basically good will lead us into the new millennium…the thousand years of peace. Serenity begins in each one's heart and mind. Start in your own "little life." The outcome on our earth depends upon the souls in it. Acceptances of the many "faces," "races," and "places" of God Goddess will lead us to harmony.

Everyone has a certain level of understanding in their knowledge of the world. Can we respect each other's ideas and allow them to perceive and worship as they will? We all are exactly where we are supposed to be. Listen to your hearts, let them open to the limitless possibilities and truths of this universe. When words no longer act as swords, we can understand the meaning of "letting them live as one people, One Spirit."

It is time to allow each one their level of understanding. If it happens not to be your way, then So Be It! There are as many paths to God as there are people, each in their own beautiful way.

TRANSFORMATION

Transformation is levels of understanding.
As we dig deep, we see more and more of our
*   true self.*
We begin to unravel our soul
As layers of the onion peel reveal its heart.
Our lives are an unwrapping of the layers
That hide our True Self.
These layers are protections and prejudices,
Untruths and lies, hurts and hatred.
As we delve into the self, we find that each layer
Brings us closer to our God Self.
At the center we find the reason for our lives.
We become the essence of our true spiritual being –
Our angel of light and love.

This part of us is with us always as we travail
the path
Back to the pure reason of our existence.
The potential of the Breath of God and Creation
Is moving us with every faint whisper of
"I AM that I Am."

2002   Purity of heart starts in the soul, as when a child views the world...unblemished, sweet, and true.   The lessons we all must learn begin in childhood: our clean slate with limitless possibilities, 100% of our brain performing, and the 144,000 functions of the human "body divine" turned on!

The "real" world for us is our everyday lives. Beyond the "veil" are a million choices for good and a million right decisions.   Angels and spirit guides abound and guide our way. The pure in heart are the innocents who can for one moment glimpse eternity. When they do, they realize that each one of us is a cherished part of the Creator, one part that makes up the everlasting whole.

2003   Children live "The Word."   They play and laugh and breathe joy.   They want to find the sweetness of life. Their purity is an example for us. Their wonder in the smallest things shows us their true calling. They are the closest to Heaven.   Their spirits have remembered their true home.

They have made the choice to try it again, to try to live the perfect life.

It is time to "bless the little children" and not take it all so seriously. There is joy in every action of this world...it is all given in love.

Ninth Holy Day
January 3
Sagittarius

"Ye Are The Light Of The World."
MATTHEW 5:14

ᴄᴏ Chapter Nine ᴄᴏ

NINTH HOLY DAY: JANUARY 3

SAGITTARIUS: NOVEMBER 23 - DECEMBER 22

DISCIPLE: PHILIP

SPIRITUAL CENTER: SACRAL PLEXUS AND
THE SPINAL CORD, WHICH CONNECTS THE
SACRAL PLEXUS TO THE BRAIN
(SEE ILLUMINED)

ATTAINMENT: TO LIVE THE PATH OF
DISCIPLESHIP.

THOUGHT MEDITATION: "YE ARE THE LIGHT
OF THE WORLD." (MATTHEW 5:14)

1983   Our lives are necessary for the learning
of all people.   What one sees and understands,
another must see. What one feels, another must feel.
When enough of us understand a great truth, the rest
will receive this truth in their soul ("100th Monkey"
Theory or "Critical Mass.")

1985   All people have the light of the Creator.
Our combined light is what makes the physical sun
shine. Our body temples contain the Cosmos. The
sun, planets, and star galaxies are within. Our "life
force" energy has its Source in a pattern in the body
called "The Divine Presence (Creator), in the
Honorific Center of the Cosmos." (Jin Shin Jyutsu®)

1990   You shine as the stars in heaven. You

105

whisper the truth to me inside. You carry me when I cannot sail. You lift me when I am downtrodden. Your life fills me when I am cold. Your essence gives me freedom. Your spirit brings all life together. "Ye are the light of the world." Your very existence gives me life. Your breath fills my nostrils. As Spirit stays, my life goes on...here today, maybe tomorrow gone.

I hope to show You how I appreciate Your many gifts to me, the gifts of life and those special gifts we have tended together. Let me use those gifts (talents) to show You and the world that I love You...maybe only a sparkle of the infinite way You love me. But just that sparkle may touch someone and make them understand that You are here, right now, with us.

1991　　　The light of our hearts and minds reflects the light of the sun. The sun symbolizes the life of the universe. It controls the growth of new life forms. It changes the seed into the mighty oak. It transforms the small-self into the higher-self. When we give forth our true nature, the sun envelopes all we come in contact with. It blesses those we touch. It transforms the meanest worm into the glorious butterfly. As we grow in the light, we know our radiance reflects the sun's illustrious rays.

1995　　　Ye, in your greatest hour of truth, are the light of the world. You are God's children, who in your true nature can emulate the Father, who can step aside and allow the Father to work through you, who can so love the world that you become the very light of the world. The spiritual kingdom is at hand. The spiritual temple is within. The glorious power of Father Mother God is within you, waiting to be reached, waiting for your call, persevering at the portals of your heart and mind. God's love never faileth. All is yours, from your divine birthright. See God's power behind every action. See all working for the good.

1997   The "life wave" may separate. One way will follow the Godlike path while the other may choose to live in ignorance. As long as there is one prejudice, we cannot evolve. We are all here together and have chosen this time to be alive. It is our duty and responsibility to investigate just why we are here. What is our purpose for living this life? What lessons keep showing up again and again? Each one of us has an important gift to share.

THE HUMAN FAMILY

Here we are on one planet.
Living together, searching for peace.
Our brothers and sisters are with us.
All nations and peoples with One God.
How can we progress and maintain a higher
*   evolution?*
By willingness to cooperate and lessons of love.
We live in this tiny speck of the universe.
We are one of the billions and billions of suns
*   and stars.*

Our little planet with its vast beauty and
harmonies of nature
Can shine as our sun reflects the greater God.
How can we live in brotherhood, humanity?
What will it take to express the Divine?
Our steady, unceasing belief that there is
One God, one planet, one people
To fulfill our destiny of love and peace.

1999   We come here with an important job to do.   Let us embrace the importance of our lives...without them the world would not be fulfilled. Just think of all the lives each one of us touches and their unending stream of possibilities.   Each life is a mirror of God Goddess within...attempting to burst forth with unbelievable love and light.

Just think how much good one single life can do...a Mother Teresa, a Princess Diana, a Jesus the Christ. People live lives like that, and many a time the world does not know their names...they live in the quiet of their own hearts and minds. Let us step up to the challenge of becoming the God centered people we are meant to be. Ye are the light of the world.

2001   Every year on January 3 (or 4), the earth in its elliptical orbit around the sun comes closer to it than any other time of the year.   Instead of 93 million miles away, we come within 90 million miles. This is very symbolic, as the earth comes closer to the sun to receive more light. This is the day that the fire was started in my bedroom from the crystal in my window.

The physical demonstration of fire represents the power of the Spiritual Fire of God. God's first ray of light refracted into the seven rays of the spectrum, and all colors of the earth and heavens were fashioned. That one ray of light split into all the colors of the rainbow and created Spirit's first light.

This spiritual fire burns within us. As the mind thinks and the heart loves, this fiery passion of thought and feeling helps to manifest our desires. See the sun in the heavens and also see it represented as our heart, the life giving element that makes all things grow.

The light of the world is inside of us. It peeks through the darkness. It blazes when we love. It teaches us divinity right now. It whispers "I love you" a million trillion times in the silence. Source gives us light to lead us out of the darkness of unknowing.

"For every 'Oh Lord' of thine are a thousand 'Here am I's.'" (Sufi Prayer)

2003   We can become a perfect channel of Spirit's unending supply. We can become a great conduit for the Creator's energy within, making right all we touch and think about.

The light of the body, the face, radiates God's healing power. You can see it in the eyes. When we are old, if we are still beautiful with wrinkles and all, God's light is shining through us. Just think how many times we bless instead of curse, how many times we send a loving thought instead of a hurtful one, how many times we choose good over evil. All these choices are counted and remembered. Every thought, word, and deed is written in the "Book of God's Remembrance." Not one thought is extinguished, but it goes on to be transformed into LIGHT.

Tenth Holy Day
January 4
Capricorn

*"Let The Christ Be Formed
In You." (Me)*
GALATIANS 4:19

ᕍ Chapter Ten ᕥ

TENTH HOLY DAY: JANUARY 4

CAPRICORN: DECEMBER 22 - JANUARY 20

DISCIPLE: SIMON - BROTHER OF JAMES AND JUDE

SPIRITUAL CENTER: KNEES (SEE ILLUMINED)

ATTAINMENT: TO BECOME A WORTHY TEMPLE FOR THE CHRIST CONSCIOUSNESS.

THOUGHT MEDITATION: "LET THE CHRIST BE FORMED IN YOU." (ME) (GALATIANS 4:19)

1982 The Christ is the tree of life, where only the good fruit is given forth with tidings of love and joy. The Christ spirit forms in us as we grow in understanding and wisdom and become those qualities. Love stands forth triumphant. It shines and creates God given attributes. There is a mystic marriage between our head (the bread) and our heart (the wine). We grow into having a spiritual "communion" with the head and the heart of Jesus the Christ.

1986 The Christ is formed in us when we let go of all judgments, when we show and see only love. The personal self steps aside, and the glory of our Creator shines through. The Holy Spirit Mother brings all to our remembrance. She brings us to the wisdom necessary to allow the Christ to be formed in us. We

113

are channels of the Creator's energy, all vibrating at different levels. His/Her perfect love comes forth to crown all those we meet. Love and compassion are the keys to creating the Christ Child within.

1987   The Christ is the perfect son or daughter of God. The baby Jesus was born in the manger, the ideal child. The Christ child is within our own being in the "manger" of the inner self, the "rainbow bridge" between the pineal and pituitary glands. The seed of the Christ is within, waiting to be born.

1988   The atoms of the physical body can become light. They travel at the speed of light, forming and disintegrating, then forming again. The atoms all spin in unison, clockwise for health and counter clockwise in disease. Atoms rotate in harmony with the heart beat of the universe, in harmony with the OM which reverberates in the silence. The OM (AUM) (AMEN) is the "lost word" of the Bible which keeps all spirit in physical creation, the sound that vibrates to solidify all manifested form.

In *Autobiography of a Yogi*, Paramahansa Yogananda says: "The Comforter, which is the Holy Ghost, whom the Father will send in my name, he shall teach you all things, and bring all things to your remembrance, whatsoever I have said to you" (John 14:26). These Biblical words refer to the threefold nature of God as Father, Son, Holy Ghost (Sat, Tat, Aum in the Hindu Scriptures).

"God the Father is the Absolute, Unmanifested,

114

existing beyond vibratory creation. God the Son is the Christ Consciousness existing within vibratory creation; this Christ Consciousness is the 'only begotten' or sole reflection of the Uncreated Infinite.

"The outward manifestation of the omnipresent Christ Consciousness, its 'witness' (Rev. 3:14), is Aum (Om), the Word or Holy Ghost: invisible divine power, the only doer, the sole causative and activating force that upholds all creation through vibration. Aum the blissful Comforter is heard in meditation and reveals to the devotee the ultimate Truth, bringing 'all things to your remembrance.'" (Explanation of "Aum" and "Christ Consciousness" in *Metaphysical Meditations* by Paramahansa Yogananda)

1989 The Christ Spirit starts as a seed within each one of us. By our devotion to love and God's way, the Christ is formed within. We are traveling this road as our supreme goal in each lifetime. When the little "I am" gives way to the grand "I AM," the personal self vanishes and the Higher Self unites with the oneness of the Godhead, and then God Goddess works totally through us in love and light.

1990

THE CHRIST SEED

Oh, that perfect seed as acorn grow.
Within my lofty wings of light.
Hidden there in soil of light and darkness.
When one thought sprouts, the everlasting vine
*   shoots forth*
And forms the child, who hopes, waits,
And slowly understands that he or she
Must become the Father Mother.
To manifest the flawlessness of the seed,
It is planted with "love absolute."
Its desires and cravings are already fulfilled.
Its dreams are already answered, if they call
*   for the good.*
Its life is born to express the infinite joys
*   Source has given us*
As eternal gifts.

1991   The seed of the Christ is the love of God planted in our Spirit. It is our divine gift, birthright, and challenge. God so loved us that a part of the universal Spirit is within, making us immortal. Our minds have this awareness fade here on earth because of the vast time and experience we have all shared. One day we will remember everything. That day is when humankind will awaken to its true purpose. Jesus came to show us the perfect life, as did Moses, Buddha, Mohammed, Krishna, Lao Tzu, and all before.

The drama of life can be played to the fullest, always knowing that it is really only a moment in eternity. Make the most of it! The problems today may seem insurmountable, but they are really stepping stones on the path of learning. We can only handle them one at a time. They are all put here for a reason. Find out what the reason is, learn from it, and then there will be no repeats. When we have learned our lesson, it doesn't bother us anymore. It just drifts in and out of our lives with no emotion. Emotions are here to help us experience the duality of this planet.

EMOTIONS ARE FOR FEELING

Emotions are for feeling, feeling in and out:
Tears of sadness; cries of joy; words of anger;
*   fear as toys.*
Round and round we go.
Sometimes laughing out.
Sometimes tears inward - make for sick bones.
Emotions are for feeling. Just what is it all about?
They say our feelings create for us, express the fears,
*   explode the tears,*
Bubble with joy and laugh as the sea carries us on.
Emotions are water, ever changing within.
When brought to the surface, they can heal our bodies.
These feelings make life holy, all worth living for.
Without the joy and passion,
Just what are we here for?
Dare to feel rotten, dare to show it.

Let the misery escape, so it doesn't "eat you up inside."
Feel like hell, feel so sad.
When you don't think you can stand it another
  moment,
You're amazed as that moment passes,
And you are still here and actually "feeling" better.
When you're in it, you think there is no way out.
When you come to the other end of it,
You just might have uncontrollable laughter.
How many times has some great tragedy
Made you laugh uproariously later.
Oh, I do mean much later!
The saddest you've been is a promise of the happiest
  you'll get.
Could it be that simple?
The pendulum swings from sad to happy,
Love to hate, anger to acceptance,
Fear to courage, and worry to trust.
The mysteries of emotion… just what are they
  here for?
The spark that ignites the passion
Can become the flame of unconditional love.
The delight of expectancy,
Brings us our child within.
Complex emotions are running around inside of us.
Without them life is flat, dull, middle ground.
The middle way is the path of the Buddha…
Not too hot, not too cold.
Lukewarm isn't so good either.

Life means feeling.
This body is here for touch, touch of skin and touch
    of hearts.
Love is here to feel…all around,
The love is here to feel.

"Life has meaning only in the struggle. Triumph or defeat is in the hands of the Gods. So let us celebrate the struggle!" (Swahili Warrior Song)

Although the evil of the world gathers force, the "devil" comes from the darkness of our own soul. We choose to create evil or transmute it to goodness and light. The "devil" is within you, as God is within you. There is only one power of the universe, the power of God Goddess. It is man's choice to use it for good or evil. God's power is supreme. In the physical we have separation, good and bad, hot and cold. We make decisions to do what our "little self" desires. In the grand scheme of things, we become our own angel or devil. We can live in the light and the light will be with us. We can choose evil and evil will haunt us. Remember, we choose to use the one power, God's power, for good or evil. Only God's law governs this universe. Disobey the law and you will have to repay the debt. Do good works and the mighty angels will be by your side. You are the great judge for yourself and know when you have transgressed the Law of Love.

119

1992   Let the Christ Child of Love be formed in me. Let His essence of life unfold in me. May His dream of the perfect life guide my being. Let His love embrace me and help me understand the beauty I AM. Let His light so shine that it illuminates my heart and my mind to appreciate and love in balance. Let the Child within become the reflection of the good Lord, to always and in all ways win with love. Let God's vision of the perfected world unfold before us. Let the love of the Christ be born within each one of us so that there is peace on earth. Let the love God has for us shine on each one of our faces and light our beings from within.

"Let the blessings of God rest upon me (you). Let His peace abide in me. Let His presence illuminate my heart, now and forever more." (Sufi Song)

1993   Jesus is our elder brother. He is the Christ of this Earth, the first to resurrect His physical body. What He did, all men and women will do. He came to show the way to truth. The "only begotten Son of God" means that the Spirit of the Father worked entirely through the man Jesus. The Spirit of Love is the only reason we are alive.

We are chosen as representatives of the voluminous faces and beings of God. As my daughter Hallae says, "God likes variety." We are blessed to be part of this divine mystery. We can champion our position and exalt our true nature as the Christ is formed in us. God took the time to create us, and now, take the time to know why.

1995   Let the spirit of love be formed in everyone so that we may fulfill our destiny of peace on earth. Let us be free to do good works and have Spirit reveal the truth. We co-create our divinity and destiny. Our thoughts of love or damnation are carried to those we think about. We are forever linked with the people we love or hate. As givers of love, we can manifest a new heaven and a new earth. The practice of brotherhood and sisterhood will emulate the angels who watch over us. We will become angels on earth as we impart our divinity and humanity to each other, learning to honor and respect our glorious uniqueness. There is good and evil in all. When we fill ourselves with unconditional love and benediction for all, we will have heaven on earth. "I can't believe Heaven could be any better than this earth." (My mother, Margie Battles)

1997   We basically act out what we see around us. It takes a progressive soul to be able to break away from his family and social norm. It takes great courage to move onward and upward and not accept the prejudice and wrong action that one's family continues to reenact. It is one who is ready to move on that creates a new life pattern and transforms heredity. "Heredity can be transformed, there are no limitations placed on anyone." (Mary Burmeister, Jin Shin Jyutsu®)

1999   Even the Father's favorite Son had to suffer at the hands of His accusers. Jesus accepted

God's will as supreme. He even asked, in the Garden of Gethsemane, "May this cup be taken from me?" (Mark 10:35) He was so alone there in His human moments of doubt. As He accepted His fate, being nailed to a cross, He said to the Court, "You would have no authority over Me if it had not been given to you from above..." (St. John 19:11) He understood that even His death was "allowed" by the Mighty hand of God as a necessary step to the resurrection.

His example has become the Star of Bethlehem. This star appears in the aura of a Christed being. There are many trials and tribulations to reach this divine position. Jesus and Mother Mary came to show us the way.

The truth of our divinity is written in our hearts and souls. The memory of every event is recorded in our bones. The truth of our "Oneness" is our only salvation and the way to conquer all fear.

Dear God: Let me be a light to all I meet. With helping hands and heart, let me show the world Your infinite love. Let me be like Your Son, who showed us the way to humility and devotion. My heart is opening to the possibility of true unconditional love. Let me be ever vigilant in my quest for truth. Let Your wisdom dawn on me like each new day. Let me know You as my Father and Mother and be the child You are proud of. Let me have an understanding countenance as I express Your life in me. Thank You for my many gifts!

2000   The Christ grid has been repaired,

making it possible for every human on the planet to reach his/her true self - a child of God. Each one has the potential to become part of the Trinity of Love: Father, Son or Daughter, and Holy Spirit Mother. The Mother is the wisdom of God, the truth made manifest. Mother heals all wounds, gives knowledge, nurtures, and blesses all. Welcome the Trinity into your lives and hearts.

2001   Jesus said in the book *The Mystical City of God*, "Just as I have told you that who knows Me knows also My Father, so I now tell you that he who knows My Mother knows Me." Mother Mary is a shining star, the loveliest flower of Heaven. She came as the pure vessel of the Christ Spirit. She, as mother, loved Him with the love of the Divine Spirit. Her mission, when accomplished, provided us with the example of God in flesh. Her continued devotion to us blesses all of us at every moment. She has attained what Jesus attained but in a different way. It is time to look to them both for guidance.

Mother Mary is a gift to us, the Queen of Heaven, the mother of all Her Children. Her innate beauty and lovingness caress our souls, bless our heads, and touch our feet. She is a kind mother who always cares even when the child has done wrong. When confessing your misgivings to Her, She answers with a kind, true blessing. Even though you may be ashamed for what you have done, Her heart is so pure that you still have the courage to tell Her. Her reprimand may be harsh but given with such great love that you can bear to hear it.

She will give you Her mantle of hope and praise and trust that you wear it wisely. She once told a seer, "Don't pray to Me, but ask Me to help you pray to the Father. We together will pray to God." Ask Her with an open, loving heart, and She will answer as a loving mother does.

2002   Somehow all of us, combined, form the "Great Body of God." The earth, the planets, and billions of stars are all expressions of "The One." In this unfathomable variety lies the biggest secret: Everything is God made manifest!

2003   Let the Spirit arise and blossom. It is time for its fruition. Learn to put your fears aside. The choices you made in the past have come to their bidding and have come to the time of manifestation. Your dreams are ready to materialize. All those long hours of work and learning must be shared. It is your job to create joy, to lift the hearts of those around you. Be at peace, and go with the flow!

Eleventh Holy Day
January 5
Aquarius

"Ye Are My Friends."

JOHN 15:4

～ Chapter Eleven ～

ELEVENTH HOLY DAY: JANUARY 5

AQUARIUS: JANUARY 20 - FEBRUARY 19

DISCIPLE: MATTHEW

SPIRITUAL CENTER: THE TWO LOWER
LIMBS (SEE ILLUMINED)

ATTAINMENT: THE PATH OF LOVE FULFILLS
EVERY LAW.

THOUGHT MEDITATION: "YE ARE MY
FRIENDS." (JOHN 15:4)

1984   Water quenches thirst…it brings life
and energy to all living things. We must become the
"water bearer" to bring nourishment to all people.
When we look to others, we are really looking at
ourselves. If we are annoyed by someone's actions, we
can be sure that we are recognizing something in them
that reminds us of our own failings. The degree might
not be the same, but if we "see it" we "own it." Each
one is a mirror of his own reflection.

1985   God wants us to look at each other and
see that you are just like me, each one a different spark
of the infinite, each one holding a treasure of love.

FRIEND

Friend, I love your heart…all you express.
You are part of me.
Your smile meets mine.
You say what I like to hear.
I meld with your laughter and your tears.
We are friends, and I can count on you to warm
* my heart,*
Even when I'm feeling blue.
You desire the things I do.
I want to hear your words are wisdom.
Our minds are alike,
And with every breath, like the wings of the lark,
I need to say, "I love your heart."

"A friend knows the song in my heart and sings it to me when my memory fails." (Donna Roberts)

1990   I look to you and say, "Ye are my friends." I see God in every one of you. I honor His presence in your Temple of the Divine. I speak to you with loving kindness. I treat you as my sister and brother. I trust that my love will be returned in kind. I know that your spirit and mine are one. I believe that our power and intention can change the world. I have faith that the new world of peace is coming. I witness the forces of God at work bringing about this harmony…harmony out of chaos. I see that the world of strife and hate has no place in the divine plan. I love you and with this serenity, look to all of you as my friends.

1993   Jesus considered everyone His friend. It did not matter who they were, what they looked like, or what they did. He simply loved them. He was so wise, with a benevolent Fatherly wisdom, that He took people under His wings of love. He was so immense in understanding that His love encompassed the world.

When Jesus was condemned, He rose above the tumult of hatred and would not participate in it, but instead sent out blessings and forgiveness. He answered hate with love and condemnation with knowledge, trying to heal and witness to the all embracing love of His Father God. After He was gone, He sent the Holy Spirit Mother... the Comforter...to shower the disciples with wisdom.

Jesus drove out the demons in those afflicted, healing those who were ready to accept the love of God. He spoke in parables to explain the simplicity and complexity of God. Each story was understood on one level by all, then on a deeper level by a chosen few. We are to look to Him in order to understand the process we must all go through to become the Christ. Our hearts must be blameless, gentle as a lamb, but strong as a lion. We are told to listen to our hearts and our desires to know how we truly are. If we reflect on the heart of Jesus, we will know all the answers.

Our world is heading toward the day when the

cross will be buried or transmuted into the fire of Spirit. The cross is our physical body with arms outstretched. It was our promise to take on the material world. It will be our destiny to transform the physical body to that of Spirit here on earth. Our lives will be as one, all knowing our Unity in Spirit. "He will wipe away every tear from their eyes. There will be no more death or mourning or crying or pain...." (Revelation 21:1)

1994 Each friend is a treasure, a brother or sister to help us along the way, a gift to share. A moment of true friendship is a blessing of love that the good Lord gives us. Each friend is a jewel that sparkles and grows. Each friend has a different function in our life. Some are like family and some are for fun, nothing serious. A true friend will listen to it all. I have been blessed with some loyal friends who have helped me through my difficult times. They have helped me at my worst, and believe me, it was not easy to listen. They have stood by me and cared in my darkest time, laughed and cried with me, loving through it all.

1995 God knows all of His children. Each one has the potential of the greatest man/woman. Each one is a perfect flower, a diamond in the crown of life. Our earthly sojourn is given as a gift, an opportunity to learn the lessons of Spirit. Each person is placed in this magnificent puzzle to work out exactly what he/she needs to learn.

We are all so much more than we can see. Some can see more than others. Use your discernment and trust them until you can see for yourself.

When you look to ones who you feel are great teachers, you may feel their power because they are powerful. Discernment comes when you awaken to see if they are using their power for good or evil.

1997   Everyone has a story of hardship and extreme joy. To one it may seem an awful life, a devil's existence. On the inner level, that person may be learning lessons we are afraid to even look at. In His almighty mercy, God gives us just what we need and only what we can handle. When you feel like you are about to break, Spirit steps in and shields you to light your way. In the darkest hour loving hands are there guiding you to explore even the darkness. Following the darkest night comes the brightest day. The pendulum swings, and for that great sorrow we receive the opposite joy.

In our sleeping state, we return to Spirit to be healed and held in the mighty arms of Heaven. The ancients knew that when we sleep, we heal. Ask God to heal you as you sleep. The Spirit never sleeps but continues to work on all the necessary details of our waking lives.

We are blessed with our friends around us. Many lose their "blood family" and see friends as their brothers and sisters. How else can it be? The love you feel can never be broken. The kindnesses live on as part of your heart and soul. The wishes for goodness and success keep on going. Always greet a stranger as a friend. They may become part of your heart.

1999 "Ye are the Light of the World." The opposing forces would have us believe in doom. I say, believe in LIGHT! Dream the seeming impossible dream into manifestation. There is a divided camp on Earth: those who speak of evil, gloom, and inevitable destruction of this planet. I say, dream of love and peace and work toward it in your life. It can be done! With all our combined prayers we can stop war! Some of the why's and how to's are up to the Divine Spirit. It is our job to see truth, to flow into God's will, and to believe there can be peace.

REMEMBER THE EARTH

Remember the earth, when it was new?
Loving and caring as we grew,
Grew in heart and soul and mind,
Accepting each other as divine.
Our spirits were free as the dove,
Gliding and searching far above.
Searching the heavens, letting no sin.
The Lord told us to look within.
There we found creation;
There we found love.
Our hearts were in heaven,
But not heaven above.

2000   We are in heaven, but just don't know it. You say heaven, here on earth? How can that be with famine, killing, disease, disharmony? All of these conditions are for a purpose. It has been a difficult lesson for us humans. We started as slaves and have now gained our freedom, but are not yet released from the bondage of the mind. It is time to fly! Let those moments of love in your life multiply. Call upon those moments when in fear. Redeem the bonuses you have earned by right living. "It is the time for all good people to come to the aid of each other."

The doom sayers are doom seers. Let us see the world as we choose to see it.   Let us see the waters clean, the earth rich with life-giving nutrients, healing foods for all people, animals, and plants, the air abundant with oxygen and life giving ethers (Chi), the "fires" burning brightly to cleanse and show the way. Start with our own life and dreams. The phoenix will rise out of the ashes, reborn. Know it, see it, believe it…heaven on earth will come. The Cosmos lives inside each one of us. Treat her with respect and she will do the same for you. "Whatsoever you do to the least of My brethren, you do it to Me…." (John 4:35)

2004   As I sit here, love goes out from me in an interconnectedness to all kingdoms of earth and the heavens. I see the oneness of all of us: human, angelic, deva, animal, plant, and mineral. I can see our union as one affecting the other, as one string pulled or pawn taken, all connecting us together in the "One Body of God." All are linked within the inbreathing and the outbreathing of the universe. All are one pulse, the heartbeat of us joined with the heartbeat of the earth. One becomes the other. All life is One in the mind of God.

We truly are brothers and sisters in light. We can become friends as we work together for the good, as we care for one another as a part of ourselves. PEACE ON EARTH and goodwill to all the kingdoms of our beautiful Mother Earth!

Twelfth Holy Day
January 6
Pisces

"The Many Faces Of God"

"I Am That I Am." EXODUS 3:14
"So God Created Man
In His Own Image." GENESIS 1:27

ᨀ Chapter Twelve ᨀ

TWELFTH HOLY DAY: JANUARY 6 - EPIPHANY

PISCES: FEBRUARY 19 – MARCH 20

DISCIPLE: PETER

SPIRITUAL CENTER: FEET (SEE ILLUMINED)

ATTAINMENT: TO BECOME THE GODLIKE
MAN AND WOMAN. OUR GLORIFIED
BODIES BECOME THE WEDDING GARMENT
TO SPIRIT.

THOUGHT MEDITATION: "I AM THAT I AM."
(EXODUS 3:14) "SO GOD CREATED MAN IN
HIS OWN IMAGE." (GENESIS 1:27)

1981   The glorified body is our Higher Self or God Self. The wedding garment weds us to Father Mother God. We become reunited with our Eternal Self. We are made in God's image to express the infinite qualities and beauty of our Creator. In the physical state we may turn away from Spirit, but the cosmic pattern inside of us knows and understands all.

1982   God's creation was fulfilled by creating man in His own image. It is our divine mission to complete His manifestation by making all things Holy. His promise is of eternal life with the Lord and all the angels. God's presence is what makes us alive. His blessings are within, waiting to blossom forth.

Our worries and cares are only a lack of faith. His

pledge to us of abundance and perfection is already within…all we have to do is claim it.

1984   We gather unto us all the lessons of life. Our physical bodies convey those lessons of love. Each cell is either in harmony or else it has the "life force" blocked, which leads to disease. Our unexpressed attitudes and emotions create the disorder in our beings.

Every atom within contains the pattern of the whole; the hologram tells that secret. The seed of perfection, the Christ, has its blueprint on every cell…the pattern of Total Love. The force of the splitting atom shows us the power of God's love in demonstration. Just think of all the blessings that could be released if this was used for the Good.

1985

KNOWING GOD

I pray to know You, God,
To feel or see one minute glimpse of Your presence,
Though You are in me, through me,
Though You are all around me,
Filling the entire universe and eons of time and
    space.
Your radiance fills, yet is born anew at each
    moment.
I pray to see one spark, to feel one touch
Of Your mighty hands that hold
The cosmos and me together as one.
Am I worthy to see the truth?

Am I capable of a glimpse of understanding?
Is "Your Divinity" alive somewhere within me?
Am I not living to express Your being?
Am I not alive to prove Your existence?
*My form, though a temporary home, has been
    frozen in time and space.*
*My immortal spirit is caught for a time in the
    body.*
When will I fly free again?
When will my wings
Fly free in Your mighty heavens?
When can I feel Your presence in and through me?
When will I know the truth of Your existence?
Can it be at that time we call death,
When death frees us to take up our spirit bodies,
And once again feel at home?
Home, being in total union
With all creations of God.
In spirit we see the wholeness.
We know that we are part of the one universe,
Under one God Supreme power.
That moment of death will be a birth
Into our real home of Spirit, Love, and Law,
God's Law of Love.

1986   "I AM that I Am."…I AM the Father
Mother, that you may be the sons and daughters of
God. "I AM…" is the God aspect. "…that I Am" is the
personal self aspect. "I AM that I Am" means God's

power in eternity helps to create the I Am of myself. God's perfection can be in and through us. When His light shines, we show love, only love.

1987   The cosmic pattern of man is made in our Creator's image. The miraculous efficiency of our physical body is a reflection of the divine workings of Spirit. We have the potential for the God man/woman right here on Earth. Our spirit is that perfection. We must learn to glorify our physical bodies, transform each cell, so that we eventually take them with us at the transition called death. The 144,000 functions of the 72,000 nerves, left and right, will be operating in full power and harmony. Every function will be turned on, creating "Homoluminous"…the divine being each truly is. "Let go, let God" do His beautiful work.

1989   When in harmony, man's body is the expression of a living dynamo with remarkable powers of efficiency, latitude, transmutation, computation, elimination, regeneration, systematization, and collaboration. Our bodies exemplify the ideal running machine, the ideal computer.

The fact that a cut or wound can heal up is itself a miracle. It's as if magic is being performed. Our bodies have the ability to heal that way on the inside, with all the millions of cells working to create new life. Every organ is a replica of a higher ideal archetype. Each one brings us a universal lesson and teaches us through attitudes and emotions.

1991

OH, CHILD

*Oh, child, scared child, child of the past, child still
    within…*

Small, helpless, a sponge soaking up everything,

Taking whatever is said as truth:

You're a good boy.

You're a bad girl.

We wanted a son. You were supposed to be a girl.

*Where have we gone wrong to deserve a brat
    like you.*

Obey me. I am King. I command you.

   I am Queen.

Listen and obey and do as I say,

Or your father will get you,

Or your mother will hit you,

Or you'll never amount to anything unless you obey.

Or ignore me or I'll ignore you,

Or I'll hit you or spank you

Or beat you, or molest you.

Love and hate rolled into one,

Helpless, innocent, like a little computer,

Taking everything in,

Taking everything as truth.

Mommy told me this, so it must be true.

I'm bad, I'm stupid, I'm good for nothing.

I will never amount to anything.

Small little child, how can we change things…

To see you as you were,

To bring you to us now,
To love you, caress you,
Tell you how much we love you,
Stroke you, defend you, adore you.
Each child has the potential for the greatest life,
If led with love, knowledge, truth,
Wisdom, strength, gratitude, and health.
All this is possible as Mommy and Daddy
Tell you and show you that
You are loved.

1993   We are sent here on a mission of growth. We act and hopefully learn what we are sent here to do. We have been delivered onto this planet, by choice, to learn the ways of God. God looks through our eyes. He feels through our hands. He walks with our feet. Our joys are His joys, our sorrows, His grief. Our triumphs bring us one rung closer to the Almighty Spirit.

When we think and image the good, the loaves will be multiplied. With intention, image it; then ask our Creator for the good of all, and it will materialize from the ethers of universal substance. The energy there is of total abundance.

Mother Earth is crying, screaming, kicking us to change. Mother Nature is a reflection of what we are going through. Every earthquake, storm, hurricane, and volcano is created by the fierce emotions of the people. The wind is mental, water is emotional, earth is physical, and fire is spirit. What goes on in the wind, water, and fire settles in earth, and thus also in our bodies. We cannot ignore the signs. The earth is rebelling because we as her people are growing and trying to throw off what is not necessary, for our survival. As we poison the earth, we poison ourselves.

We are living in a time of tremendous change. Earth is changing, the water and temperatures are changing, our physical bodies and our DNA are transforming. (There have been children and adults who have started to multiply their strands of DNA!) The fire is exploding from the center of the earth. The fire that gives us life is spitting out all that is unneeded.

Wake up! The same natural disasters that we see are indicative of what is going on in each one of us. Clean up the emotions, the mental picture, the physical body, and the soul. The soul is the sum total of all our experience and karma, in all of our lives. Clean it all up or it will be exploded from the volcano into the sky and onto another planet where war still exists.

Wake up! Don't look to others to see their faults. Pay attention to your own. Don't compete with others. Instead set your own goals of achievement. Start right here! We know not the hour that death comes. "I come as a thief in the night." Be prepared!

1999 "In My own image, I created you. I fashioned you to experience joy, in every aspect of your lives. It has been My wish for you to be healthy and prosper...to live full and abundant lives. It has been My dream for you to express beauty and light...to ease each other's way.

"It is time to live in brotherhood, to stop your fighting and quarreling...to cease destroying your planet with bombs and poisons that fill your air, water, and earth. It is time to stop living a selfish life of greed and to begin respecting the wonders I have provided for you.

"It is your mission to create a new Heaven and a new Earth. The possibilities are all here. What will you do with the beautiful lives I have given you? How will you use your precious time, and energy? Every action is given with love. When you are chastised, it is to help balance out your learning. The dream of peace on Earth is very present in your consciousness...start living it NOW! Each one of you can change the world in your own special way!"

2001   In God's image, I Am created and in that likeness, my life unfolds. In His/Her mind, I am formed from the heavens and the earth. Every particle of earth and the stars are within my body Temple Beautiful. It is time to recognize our worthiness, our very important part of the divine plan.

The message is clear: Be humble and follow the narrow middle path, the path of righteousness less traveled. Our journey has been repeated many times, falling off and then rising to the summit. There are so many layers to who we are. Behold a new life!

Our "shadow self" emulates our own darkness. Our fears are drawn to us to be experienced. As our darkness is brought to the surface, it too grows from under the ground to search for the light of the sun. Our faults must be owned to be healed. How many times have we been unkind, said a harsh word or stupid joke that hurt someone's heart? How often have we cursed at strangers and those we supposedly love? How much would we give to help another one in trouble? How would we live if we, too, were in bondage, in a physical, emotional, and mental prison of our own making? How many times have we laughed at someone's stupidity, growled or barked when we were angry, or cowered in fear of the unknown? Have we worried for eons for what might be, or cried an ocean of tears for lost loves or other things? How many times have we shown a brave face when inside we were dying? How many hours have we "tried to" do this or that, to no avail?

All of this pain provides the opportunity to choose the highest road. Lessons come to us each day, each moment. Will we recognize them for what they are, or will we faint at the sight of them? Everything that is happening to us is by choice...God's choice and ours. Take heart and follow that gentle thing called Love. It will lead you to the Spirit within. It will unlock doors never imagined. It will free your soul!

2003 January 6 is called "Epiphany" and "Little Christmas." It honors the coming of the three

145

Wise Men to the baby Jesus. It is the time to spend inside our hearts, to be with "The One." It is the time to give of our love and devotion to the Christ Spirit as our goal, our goal of love. We wait for the moment that the Christ Child is born within us. The Christ is King, the King or Queen of Love...all else pales at the Great Presence. All questions are answered, hopes fulfilled. Boundless joy can be ours for the asking, "the peace that passeth all understanding." (Philippians 4:7) Wait for the Christ to enter and blossom and grow. Be at peace, and all shall be answered.

2004 The light comes to us when we are ready. It shines from us as we evolve in our understanding of the whole picture. There are so many facets to God and His universe. How could we know it all? It is timeless and spaceless, all infinity wrapped into one soul. Each life is a pattern, looking for the good. Each one is a blessing, some in disguise.

Wait for Spirit and She will come. It is our destiny to know who we really are. It is our message to share our knowledge with those we meet. It is time for all of us to step back and see the divine spark that ignites our souls, to search more for the meaning of it all. It seems so random; this is the illusion of this world. Each step we take is acknowledged as another opportunity for union with our Creator within.

THE MANY FACES OF GOD

I look upon the many faces of God,
And in each one is the Holy Breath.
Within each one shines the spark of divinity.
His hands lie invisibly
Resting upon each shoulder.
He has written us upon the palms of
  His hands.
Within each form is the perfect seed of
  perfection,
Waiting to blossom and grow.
The Lord has as many faces
As there are grains of sand,
Drops of water in the ocean,
Shifts of wind through the air,
Flames of fire to heat and destroy.
His light is behind each one of our faces.
Some shine bright as a million stars,
Some are glowing even at night,
Each one's existence dependent on the eternal
  life within.
As we look at the many faces of God,
Remember, we are looking at ourselves,
Because as God is, we are… one.
Oneness. United. Eternally One.

TWO SUNS

Merry Christmas!

And a Happy New Year!

VISION OF PEACE

I will hold the vision of peace,
Not judging by appearances.
I will trust the Holy promises
Of the coming Golden Age.
It will take great fortitude and faith
To continue my vision,
In the seeming turmoil of this earth.
My promise is to bring harmony out of chaos
And be the peacemaker in my world.
This will grow from my little center of being,
To touch all those around me.
From here it will create a wave
Which will touch all people.
And all hearts and minds will be united
In the NEW WORLD OF PEACE.

About the Author

Merry C. Battles LMT, has worked in the Healing Arts since 1977. She began her career working in a salon in Los Angeles frequented by Hollywood Celebrities. Merry learned massage at Louise Long Studio. Louise Long was a Physical Therapist who developed the art of reshaping the body and smoothing out cellulite in the 1930's. Many of the old stars of Hollywood and the current stars receive these treatments.

Merry has always approached her work as a healing tool. She has practiced the Art of Massage, Cellulite Massage, Jin Shin Jyutsu® (ancient Japanese Acupressure), CranioSacral Therapy, Reiki, and Foot Reflexology.

Merry is a Continuing Education Provider for Massage Therapists in the State of Florida. She teaches two introductory classes in Jin Shin Jyutsu®. Her classes are open to all people. Merry has also been a frequent public speaker in the area for the past four years.

She has published art, poetry, and writing in "Sedona – Journal of Emergence," "Connecting Link," "InnerSelf Publications," "Natural Awakenings," among others.

Merry has been a student of the ancient spiritual mysteries for as many years. Her greatest joy in life is to learn about the spiritual. This is reflected in all of her work.

Printed in the United States
29392LVS00001B/115-183

9 781420 815719